OUR STRUCTURE

Carrying Out the Vision

Brian H. Hughes

Augsburg Fortress
Minneapolis

OUR STRUCTURE
Carrying Out the Vision

Developed in cooperation with the Division for Congregational Ministries of the Evangelical Lutheran Church in America, Michael R. Rothaar, project manager.

Portions of this book are adapted from *Developing Effective Committees*, by Michael R. Rothaar, ©1993 Augsburg Fortress.

The "Keys to Hospitality" tool on pages 87-89 is adapted from *Shaping Ministry for Your Community*, copyright © 1993 Augsburg Fortress.

Scripture quotations are from New Revised Standard Version Bible, copyright © 1989 Division of Christian Education of the National Council of the Churches of Christ in the United States of America. Used by permission.

Series overview: David P. Mayer, Michael R. Rothaar
Editors: Laurie J. Hanson, Andrea Lee Schieber, James Satter

Cover design and series logo: Marti Naughton
Text design: James Satter
Cover photograph: Gordon Gray, FRPS

About the cover image: The centerpiece of the Resurrection Window in First Lisburn Presbyterian Church, Northern Ireland, was created by stained glass artist James Watson, Belfast, from fragments of church windows destroyed by a car bomb in 1981 and restored after a second bomb in 1989. The window symbolizes new life in Christ, which transforms darkness to light, hatred to love, despair to hope, and death to life. The members of First Lisburn Presbyterian have lived out this promise through new initiatives for community service, reconciliation, and peace-making.

ISBN 0-8066-4407-9

The paper used in this publication meets the minimum requirements of American National Standard for Information Sciences—Permanence of Paper for Printed Library Materials, ANSI Z329.48-1984.

Manufactured in the U.S.A.

06   05   3   4   5   6   7   8   9   10

✚ Contents

Series Overview

Welcome to the Congregational Leader Series, and welcome to the journey of discovering God's future for you and your congregation. Your congregation's mission and ministry are given to you by God. We sometimes refer to "our church," but it is always Christ's church. We are at best its stewards or caretakers, not its owners. As we plan, organize, and lead, we strive toward excellence in everything we do to reflect the glory and grace of God, who has entered human life to redeem us.

As a congregational leader, you may be asking, "What is our mission? How should we structure things? How can we plan for the future and where will the resources come from?" The Congregational Leader Series provides resources for effective planning and leadership development. Each book includes biblical and theological foundations for planning and leadership development, and practical information to use in building on your congregation's strengths.

We are first of all called to be faithful to God's word and will. Exploring the Bible enables us to discern what God's plan is for us as individuals and as a congregation. Ignoring or minimizing the centrality of God in our deliberations risks not only failure but also our faith. In the words of the psalmist, "Unless the LORD builds the house, those who build it labor in vain"(Psalm 127:1).

Why should we engage in congregational planning and leadership development? When the congregation is at its best, these activities aid us in fulfilling our mission to the world: reaching out with the gospel of Jesus Christ. Faithful planning for mission mirrors God's activity in the world, from creating and covenant-making to gathering and renewing the church. When congregations fail to plan, they risk dissipating the resources they have been given by God and begin falling away from all that God has intended for them.

In short, faithful planning and leadership development engage the congregation and all its members in the creative work of God. Continually analyzing and shaping our vision, mission, ministry, and context allows us to ask, "What is God calling our congregation to be?" Working to develop and support leaders enables us to ask, "How has God gifted each of us for ministry?"

We begin with prayer

As congregational leaders, we always begin our endeavors with prayer. Discerning God's will for us is a task that requires that we be in communication with God. Unfortunately, we often come up with new ideas and programs—and then pray that God will bless them! That order needs to be reversed. Our prayers should precede our plans, helping us discern God's call to us.

In his few years of public ministry, Jesus accomplished a tremendous amount of healing, teaching, and service for others. However, his ministry did not begin until after he had spent an extended period of time in the wilderness reflecting on his call and God's purpose for his life. Following that retreat, virtually every moment of his life's story was punctuated with prayer and ultimately concluded with his supplications in Gethsemane and on the cross.

Paul wrote to the Thessalonians, "Rejoice always, pray without ceasing, give thanks in all circumstances; for this is the will of God in Christ Jesus for you" (1 Thessalonians 5:16-18). These words were meant for us—congregational leaders anxious to get on with things that need to be done. Notice how Paul places *prayer* between *rejoice* and *thanks* in this verse. Prayer is not simply another task to be done nor an obligation to be met. It is a gift of God to be celebrated and used with joy and thanksgiving. It is meant to permeate our lives. As leaders, we are seeking to construct God's will in our communities. God invites us to build with gladness and to make prayer the mortar between every brick we lay.

As congregational leaders, we always begin our endeavors with prayer.

We build from strength

Most leadership resources begin with the assumption that there is a problem to be solved. In the midst of the real problems that surround us, however, our task as congregational leaders is to identify the strengths, giftedness, and blessings that God has given to us and the congregation. Our primary calling is not to be problem-solvers but to be asset-builders. Paul reminds us, "Let all things be done for building up"(1 Corinthians 14:26). This is not license to ignore problems, conflicts, or deficiencies. Rather, it is a call to view the brokenness around us in a new way.

> **Our primary calling is not to be problem-solvers but to be asset-builders.**

Our role as Christian leaders is to attempt to look at our congregation, our fellow Christians, and ourselves, as God sees us. "This is my commandment, that you love one another as I have loved you" (John 15:12). Jesus did not blindly ignore the problems around him. Instead, he viewed those problems through a lens of love, appreciation, and forgiveness. We are called to build from strength, to construct our plans and visions from what God has given us. When we try to build from weakness and focus only on our problems, we compound both and ultimately fail.

First Church was located in a growing, well-to-do suburb, on a main thoroughfare, and in a beautiful new building. The members of First Church appeared to have everything going for them, and the congregation's future looked very bright.

The congregation, however, faced an ongoing problem with mortgage payments. This problem became so all-consuming that the congregation began to lose sight of its strengths, gifts, and mission for the future. The members of First Church had everything they needed to solve the problem of mortgage payments but they were unable to stop fixating on it. Soon, many other issues surfaced as everyone became a fault-finder.

Today there is no mortgage-payment problem because there is no First Church. The preoccupation with weakness and deficiency blinded the congregation to the reality of its gifts. This congregation died, not because of its problems but because of its perspective.

We must constantly ask ourselves and others, "Where is God at work here? What gifts have we received for ministry in this place?" Focusing only on what we don't have breeds jealousy, competition, hopelessness, and lost vision. Focusing on our gifts gives birth to joy, affirmation, and hope.

We won't find quick fixes

We live in a culture obsessed with quick fixes and mesmerized by the notion that there is a prescription for every ailment and accident. But things keep falling apart. People get sick. Programs fail. Committees don't function. Plans backfire. And goals aren't met. The list of mistakes, failures, misfires, and flops grows and grows. In his letter to the Romans, Paul reminds us that "all have sinned and fall short of the glory of God"(Romans 3:23). Paul says this not to weigh us down with despair, but instead to remind us that our salvation comes from God and not ourselves.

Faithful leaders have a deep respect for the reality of problems and obstacles. Things will always fall apart. That's why planning, assessing, goal-setting, leading, and visioning are ongoing processes, not quick fixes. As leaders, we need to know the nature of sin and publicly acknowledge its pervasiveness. Then we can lead, not with unhealthy fatalism, but with honesty, humility, and a sense of humor.

We are all ministers

As Christians, everything we do and plan is communal. We cannot plan unilaterally or devise strategies in isolation. To be sure, each of us has received salvation individually through baptism, but at that moment, through the water and the Word, we were united with the body of Christ. Even the gifts that God has given each of us are meant for the common good of all God's people: "To each is given the manifestation of the Spirit for the common good" (1 Corinthians 12:7).

Each of us is a minister, whether pastor or lay person, and each of us is called to serve others.

In other words, each of us is a minister, whether pastor or lay person, and each of us is called to serve others. This is a radical departure from our culture's overwhelming emphasis on individual independence. The idea that we are all ministers and that as the church we minister as a community has tremendous implications for all of our planning and development efforts.

Leadership development is nothing more than equipping the members of the congregation so that they are strengthened for ministry: "The gifts he gave were that some would be apostles, some prophets, some evangelists, some pastors and teachers, to equip the saints for the work of ministry, for building up the body of Christ" (Ephesians 4:11-12). Paul would be appalled at the idea that a paid professional minister should carry out all of the ministry of the congregation or that only some people in the congregation are called to ministry.

Faithful planning and leadership development affirm that all of God's people are gifted and invited to participate in ministry. Identifying, embracing, and strengthening each other's gifts for common mission is a daunting task that never ends, but through that effort and in that journey we become what God intended: "But you are a chosen race, a royal priesthood, a holy nation, God's own people, in order that you may proclaim the mighty acts of him who called you out of darkness into his marvelous light" (1 Peter 2:9).

A model for understanding congregations

Congregations are extremely complex. Throughout the Congregational Leader Series, we invite you to look at your congregation through a particular model or set of lenses. This model helps us to understand why congregations are so complex, and it provides some important clues for the leadership skills and tasks that are needed.

A congregation resembles three different institutions at the same time: a *community of spiritual formation*, a *voluntary association*, and a *nonprofit organization*. This isn't a matter of size—the largest and smallest are alike in this. It isn't a matter of context—the model applies to both urban and rural settings. Each type of institution has different values and goals, which may even contradict each other. Each of these values and goals requires different things from leaders.

Communities of spiritual formation

A congregation is, in part, a community of spiritual formation. People come to such a community to join with others in growing closer to God. They seek to understand God's word and God's will for their life. They seek an experience of God's presence, a spiritual or emotional awareness of transcendence and love. They seek time for contemplation and prayer, and also time to work with others on tasks that extend God's love to others.

How are our congregations communities of spiritual formation? Much of congregational life centers on worship. We teach children and adults the practice of faith. The church provides support in Christ's name during times of crisis and need. We engage in visible and public activities, such as offering assistance to people who are homeless, or hungry, or survivors of abuse, as a way of both serving God and proclaiming God's mercy and justice.

The most important value in a community of spiritual formation is authenticity.

The most important value in a community of spiritual formation is authenticity. There is no room for pretense, no room for manipulation, and no room for power games. The goals we establish must be clearly directed to outcomes in people's spiritual lives. The fundamental question for self-evaluation is this: "How has our ministry brought people closer to God?"

Voluntary associations

Like any club or voluntary association, a congregation is a gathering of people who are similar to one another in specific ways, share a common purpose, and largely govern and finance their organization's existence and activities. In addition, people often find that belonging to a club is a way to make friends and social or business contacts, and enjoy meaningful leisure time activities. Some voluntary associations, such as Kiwanis or Lions clubs, have charitable purposes and sometimes seek support from people beyond their own membership. Some voluntary associations are focused on common interests or activities, such as gardening or providing youth athletic leagues.

Membership requirements may be strict or fluid, costs may be high or low, and commitments may be long or short, but they are spelled out rather clearly. A number of unwritten rules may serve to get people to conform to common values. Most voluntary associations would like to have more members, both to strengthen their organization and to expand the social benefits that come from a broader circle. But the new members usually are people who are very much like those who are already members.

The most important value in a voluntary association is effectiveness in helping people relate to one another.

The most important value in a voluntary association is effectiveness in helping people relate to one another. The goals are largely relational. There must be many opportunities for people to form relationships, especially with those with whom they have much in common. The association must operate in such a way that people all feel that their own values and hopes are being well served, usually through direct access to the decision-making process and ample opportunities for public dissent. People want and expect to be contacted regularly by both leaders and other members, and to feel that they are fully accepted as part of the group.

It is also important that there is a consensus—a shared vision—on what the association is and does. When conflict emerges, it must be negotiated and resolved. Because membership is voluntary, when there's conflict, or when they just don't feel part of the group anymore, people are usually quick to withhold their financial support or quit altogether.

Nonprofit organizations

As if it weren't complicated enough to be both a community of spiritual formation and a voluntary association, now consider that your congregation is also a nonprofit organization. It is a chartered or incorporated institution, recognized as a legal entity by the federal, state, and municipal government. A congregation can borrow and lend, sue and be sued. You as a congregation are accountable to society and responsible for following all applicable laws. Almost all congregations are property owners and employers. The congregation has formal operational procedures and documents (from your constitution to state laws) that dictate how you must make decisions and conduct your affairs. The usually unspoken but fundamental goal of a nonprofit organization is self-perpetuation, making sure that the institution will continue.

In this regard, congregations are similar to any business that offers services to the public. Being *nonprofit* simply means that the organization's assets can't be distributed to individuals or for purposes contrary to the charter. It doesn't mean that the congregation can't or shouldn't be run in a businesslike manner—or that it can't accumulate assets. The actual operation doesn't differ much from that of a profit-making business. In a nonprofit organization, the primary value is efficiency, or achieving the greatest results with the least possible expenditure of resources.

Another core value is continuity, with orderly systems that must be applied by anyone who carries out the organization's work. To reach financial goals, a nonprofit organization seeks voluntary contributions and often regularizes revenue through endowments and ancillary sources of income. Efforts are made to minimize costs without sacrificing quality. The organization also tries to build reserves to meet unanticipated circumstances and periodic needs (such as replacement of depreciating assets). Policies are in place to protect the staff and volunteers, and to ensure clear and mutually agreed upon expectations. There are clear lines of accountability and each person operates within a specified scope of decision-making.

In a nonprofit organization, the primary value is efficiency, or achieving the greatest results with the least possible expenditure of resources.

Planning in a nonprofit organization includes making the best use of property and facilities. The property is seldom an end in itself, but the goal of leadership is always to maximize its usefulness. Other organizational goals revolve around having a truly public presence, including marketing effectively, identifying the needs and wants of a particular group of people, developing a product or service that addresses those needs, and informing the target group of its desirability and availability. Nonprofit organizations must do this as surely and skillfully as those in the profit sector.

You may have heard that "you shouldn't be a manager, you should be a leader." This is unfortunate language, because management is part of leadership, and voluntary organizations need managers. How you analyze, organize, delegate, supervise, and evaluate the congregation's work is critical to its vitality.

Leadership

What does the word *leadership* really mean? Think of it as having three dimensions: *character*, *knowledge*, and *action*. *Character* permeates all three aspects of this model. Leaders have principles and try to live them out. In any of the three ways in which we're looking at congregations, leaders are honest, trustworthy, dedicated, caring, disciplined, and faithful to the core principles—and have many more virtues as well. Although everyone sins and fails, be clear that improvement is expected from all leaders.

It is not only character that counts. Leaders must also know things and do things. *Knowledge* and *action* can be developed. They can be learned in books and classes or from working with people who have expertise. Things we know from one part of our experience can be applied to other parts of our lives.

Applying the congregational model

The three-part model of congregations is helpful in exploring the different things that leaders must be, know, and do in a community of spiritual formation, in a voluntary association, and in a nonprofit organization.

Problems develop when the values, goals, and leadership styles appropriate to one part of the congregational model are mistakenly applied to one of the others. It is not wrong to value authentic spirituality, effective interpersonal relationships, and operational efficiency. There are times when each of these should be given the highest priority. Recognize that your congregation probably has emphasized one of these areas at the expense of the others, and plan your way to a better balance. Embrace the wonderful complexity of congregational life and ask God to move among us to change us and renew us and rededicate us to God's own purposes.

The Congregational Leader Series

This is one of several books in the Congregational Leader Series. The entire series seeks to build on the positive, basing your planning on assets rather than deficiencies, and to focus on outcomes, enabling your congregation to make a specific and definable difference in people's lives. The series has two sets: congregational planning and leadership development. Books in this series can be used in any order, so you can get started with those books that are most helpful for you and your congregation. The reproducible tools can be used with your council, committees, planning teams, leadership groups, and other members of the congregation. Visit www.augsburgfortress.org/CLS to download and customize these tools.

Faithful planning and leadership development take us on a journey, a pilgrimage, and an exploration of God's possibilities for you and your congregation. The Congregational Leader Series provides resources for your travels, as you seek God's will and guidance for you and your congregation.

This image of a cross indicates that further information on a topic appears in another book in the Congregational Leader Series.

Chapter 1

Carrying Out the Vision

For just as the body is one and has many members, and all the members of the body, though many, are one body, so it is with Christ. For in the one Spirit we were all baptized into one body.

—1 Corinthians 12:12-13

The meeting is set to begin promptly at 7:30 p.m. There are a few stragglers, but nearly everyone has arrived, at least physically. You look around the table, ready to begin, and then it hits you. Your fellow members are about to give you one of their most important commodities—time. Hours before one person was stuck in evening traffic, frantic that she wouldn't get home in time to pick up the kids after school. Another isn't sure his two kids really understand their homework and wonders if he made the right choice by giving up an evening for a meeting. Still another spent the day puttering around the house, eventually grabbed a leisurely dinner, and wandered over to church. Yet another is worried that this may be the week that pink slips start appearing at the office.

If the next 60 minutes are not sufficiently fulfilling to most of those present, they may make other choices next time. You're excited about the project your team has been assigned. You understand how it fits into the overall vision and mission of the congregation, but this is the moment of truth. You adjust your written agenda, look around the room, and prepare to launch into your meeting. You've heard that church committees can be a boring waste of time and seen enough of that yourself. You want this to be different. You want your participants to know and feel they are part of a team doing important work in the church. You're willing to do whatever it takes to make sure the needs of your fellow members and the tasks at hand are both engaged with creativity and commitment.

Using this book

Welcome to the joy of leadership in the church and welcome to the Congregational Leadership Series, a series designed to give you basic tools for managing the mission and ministry of your congregation.

Unless it has its roots sunk deeply into the mission and vision for a congregation, a strong emphasis on organizing can be a sign that a congregation is in deep decline. To be clear about this, without a powerful vision for the future, a stand-alone organizing process will drain the joy out of a congregation and its leaders. Do not consider how you will organize for mission and ministry until leaders are properly trained and the congregation has identified its mission and goals.

Different congregations have different needs for organizational structure. Congregations with fewer than 350 baptized members are probably best served by a less formal organizational structure. Mid-sized congregations will need a more formal structure in most cases. Congregations with more than 1500 baptized members will find useful information here—ideas that can be adapted to their particular settings—but they should also consult other books and resources that will help them make the most of their strengths.

Different congregations have different needs for organizational structure.

This book is written for congregational leaders who do part of their work through groups. These leaders include those who serve in paid

---

This book will not help you to magically patch over a declining ministry so it will stay afloat for a few more years. Organizing simply for the sake of organizing can quickly become a burden to everyone involved.

Because successful organizing occurs as part of planning and retooling a congregation's mission to meet the future, the material in this book will be most useful when read as part of a strategic planning process.

staff positions (such as pastors, associates in ministry, and volunteer coordinators) and those who are unpaid (such as officers of the congregation council). This book also might be helpful to all the people who serve as members of your congregation's planning teams, committees, task forces, or other working groups.

You may read this book on your own, but you might also read sections, or even the entirety of the text, in group planning sessions. Arriving at a shared understanding of the issues involved in organizing a group might heighten your productivity and deepen the satisfaction of group members, who will be glad they gave of something tremendously precious in our age—their time.

The material in this book can be used as part of a leadership development or training program in your congregation, synod or judicatory, or region. Some congregations conduct a systematic leadership development program for officers, council members, ministry coordinators, committee chairs, and other leaders. In some areas, workshops, seminars, and skills training for professional and lay leaders are offered for groups of congregations. Check to see what is available for leaders in your congregation. If no such programs exist in your area, you might want to take the initiative to start a program.

The role of organization in a congregation

Effective mission and ministry can happen when five things are in place in a congregation:

Vision　　　　　　　*Planning*　　　　　　　*Leadership*

　　　Organization　　　　　*Accountability*

This book highlights the role of organization and structure in fulfilling the mission and carrying out the vision for a congregation. Other books in the Congregational Leader Series can help you address vision, the strategic planning process, and leadership development.

Without the gift of vision the church as the body of Christ will wander around bumping into trees, unable to see a path through the forest of our present age. Similarly, without the gift of leadership the body of Christ won't have the energy to keep moving forward. Its "get up and go" will have "gone and went." But without the bones, without the structure, the body can't get off the ground! Without the hard, nearly inflexible skeleton, the muscles have nothing to pull against and the joints won't work. Be it muscles in the legs or the complex collection of tendons and sinews in the hand, the expected work is not produced without bones. Vision and leadership are used to determine the direction, but the bones hold things together during the expedition.

Structure plays a very specific role in the life of a congregation. When things don't go according to plan, start looking at how things are organized and managed. Without a mutually agreed upon way of making things happen, vision becomes clouded with unmet dreams and leaders become exhausted because nothing seems to happen or change. In Romans 12, Paul makes clear that there are many gifts, all of them of equal importance to the body of Christ. One of these gifts is administration, which enables a person to understand the "bones" or what makes a congregation function smoothly as it works toward fulfilling its mission and goals.

As you will discover, one set of bones doesn't fit all bodies or fit at all times. Each congregation will need to customize its structure and continue to make changes based on its specific calling for mission and ministry. This book provides you with the basic components needed to custom build a structure that will meet the needs of your particular congregation. If you were hoping for an easy fix, you're in for a disappointment. The only foundation we know for sure that's needed is faith in Jesus Christ. Nearly everything else is open for discussion!

Each congregation will need to customize its structure.

Organization in a changing world

How we've organized ministry in the past no longer seems to work. Traditional ways of organizing congregational life are breaking down as fewer people give their time to serve on committees and as membership in many mainline denominations declines. Congregational leaders are coming to the conclusion that this can't go on and that the situation must somehow be addressed. The first step toward positive change is being uncomfortable with the present. Without urgency, we don't have the sufficient emotional energy to begin and sustain any sort of change process.

Leadership and organization

Leadership is another gift that enables us to glorify God and build up the body of Christ. Those with the gift of leadership help cast a congregation's vision, establish goals, model trust, and motivate fellow believers. Leaders also help to identify times when changes in organizational structure are needed to strengthen a congregation's efforts to carry out the vision. They consider how to best hold one another accountable so that the mission and ministry of a congregation can be effective and life-giving.

Types of working groups

Experts today are re-evaluating how congregations can best organize themselves to effectively carry out their mission and ministry. Some would claim that the day of the standing committee is nearly over because volunteers aren't interested in giving the kind of time needed for committees to function well. Others believe standing committees are needed to maintain continuity and ongoing accountability. By learning and understanding the tasks and functions of working groups, you can determine which is best for your congregation or a particular mission or ministry.

Congregations can be organized with a wide variety of working groups.

Congregations can be organized with a wide variety of working groups. The working groups in your congregation might be called committees. Your congregation may have boards, which are policy-setting groups. A congregation council, board, or vestry may function as the board of directors for your congregation. There may be other boards for outreach ministries to set policies or advise a paid staff member or the congregation council.

This book uses the term *planning teams* to refer to the standing committees or groups which take responsibility for the main program areas of the congregation's life and *congregation council* to refer to a group that sets policies and oversees the work of planning teams.

A planning team or staff member may appoint a task force, which usually has a more limited scope and duration than a planning team. The youth planning team, for example, might create a task force to organize a group of young people to attend a national youth gathering. The task force might begin working a year before the gathering and finish its task as soon as the post-gathering evaluation is completed. While the youth planning team will arrange for regular progress reports, it may or may not have a member on the task force. Chapter 6 of this book discusses the mechanics of delegation to a person or group: responsibility, authority, and accountability.

A project team is a group of people drawn from several different planning teams to work toward a goal of limited scope for a limited time. The worship planning team might establish a goal of adding two contemporary Christian songs to a blended worship service. The evangelism planning team might have a goal to contact people who attend worship services for the first time within 48 hours of the visits. These two planning teams might form a smaller project team in order to simultaneously track the impact of changing music in worship and making a more rapid response to visitors. Do either of these goals independently make a difference in whether a visitor returns again or do they provide a greater benefit when linked together? The project team members would complete their work by reporting the results to the two planning teams, the pastor or assigned staff person, and the congregation council.

Still another set of working groups that contribute greatly to a congregation's ministry are those that tend to operate a bit loosely, but still represent a significant component in the organizational structure of most congregations: groups of people who take care of the altar, usher, work on relief projects such as quilting or sewing, teach Sunday school, lead small groups, sing in a church choir, and others. These groups are relatively permanent and provide direct and meaningful ways for people to offer their time and talent. They are made up of people who have found their niche in ministry and take ongoing responsibility for some aspect of the congregation's work. This book identifies these groups as *guilds* or *service groups*, although they have many names. Be sure to recognize and appreciate the considerable influence they have on the total picture of your congregation's ministry.

> There isn't only one way to organize mission and ministry in every congregation.

The freedom to fail

At the outset of any discussion concerning organization, it is important to consider a fundamental truth: the good news of Jesus Christ is a word of freedom. The gospel frees us to use our God-given gifts of vision and leadership, knowing there isn't one "right" plan or direction for a congregation or only one way to organize mission and ministry in every congregation. That's scary. That's exciting. That's what it is to live under the liberty of God's grace.

God gives leaders great dreams for mission and ministry and then sets them free to use their spiritual gifts of creativity and wisdom in crafting a plan. As a congregational leader, you need to hear again and again that the gospel sets you free to dream, experiment, risk, change, and sometimes to fail spectacularly along the way. You can do all these things because, no matter what happens, God has promised to love and support you as you pick yourself up and make another run at living out life as Jesus' disciple. Without the assurance of the gospel, our vision can be darkened with hesitancy, our leadership hampered by fear of public judgment, and the bones of our organization weakened by lack of use. Lead boldly where Christ has blazed the trail and know that you will not travel alone.

Chapter 2

Going to God with All Things

So Moses said to the Lord, "Why have you treated your servant so badly? Why have I not found favor in your sight, that you lay the burden of all this people on me? . . . If this is the way you are going to treat me, put me to death at once—if I have found favor in your sight—and do not let me see my misery." So the Lord said to Moses, "Gather for me seventy of the elders of Israel, whom you know to be the elders of the people and officers over them; bring them to the tent of meeting, and have them take their place there with you. I will come down and talk with you there; and I will take some of the spirit that is on you and put it on them; and they shall bear the burden of the people along with you so that you will not bear it all by yourself."

—Numbers 11:11, 15-17

In the book of Numbers, we learn that Moses was surrounded by unhappy people. The trip had certainly started with a lot of fanfare as the Israelites swept out of Egypt, clamoring to reach their new home. Nothing was going to stop them—not a sea, not Pharaoh's army, not the endless desert. But like human communities of all times and places, emotional excitement eventually wore thin as the reality of the real journey ahead began to sink in. The people began to complain about everything: the food was boring, the trip was taking too long, and the scenery never changed. Sleeping in tents was becoming uncomfortable, and they longed for the hot showers they'd left back in Egypt. The people turned to their leader with their unrealistic expectations: It was Moses' job to make everything happen. It was his fault the vision was running out of power. It was up to him to make sure the dream didn't die.

At this point, Moses was exhausted and overburdened. Though called by God with a powerful vision of freedom, too many demands from too many people were draining his spiritual batteries and diminishing his passion to keep pointing toward the future. He said, "Take me now, Lord!"

Dealing with the unknown that lies ahead

If to this point your congregation's journey has been uneventful, the path gentle, and the view familiar, know that this can change when a vision takes hold and a plan begins to unfold. As a leader in a congregation, you will encounter unanticipated difficulties and challenges.

As Moses discovered, it's not always possible for us to foresee the really tough dilemmas waiting ahead for a person, family, or community of faith. The Israelites had left the familiar, but had not yet arrived at the new. They had listened to their leader and risked leaving what they understood, but the journey turned out to be rougher than they had expected. The vision of freedom that enticed the people out of Egypt didn't keep them from losing heart in the wilderness.

Moses didn't have the abilities or resources to carry out the vision on his own.

At the mid-point, it seems easier to turn around and go back to what is recognizable rather than move ahead with change or transformation. This is an important moment in any organization. Many congregations slow down or end their journey at this point as they discover that vision, planning, and leadership development have not fully prepared people for new and unfamiliar territory. The actual destination is still unknown, a vision of what awaits. People may say, "We've never done it that way before," and then give up.

But God doesn't give up so easily. The vision of freedom for God's people didn't end with one individual's exhaustion. The newly freed but grumpy crowd didn't understand, but the situation helped Moses unwittingly tumble to the right conclusion. He realized that he didn't have the abilities or resources to carry out the vision on his own. Alone he couldn't carry the entire community. He needed to go to God with all things in prayer.

God responded to Moses' concerns. Now it was time to construct the framework of an effective organization. It was time to pack the bags, stow the tents, and continue the journey.

The spiritual life of a congregational leader

The Bible is about the ultimate release from bondage. As Christians, we are about sharing the gospel, a word of light and life for those who sit in darkness and the shadow of death. Sharing that gospel brings forth the most fulfilling expression of our personal gifts.

Like Moses, you can go to God with all things, seeking help and guidance as well as healthy, grace-filled ways to organize mission and ministry and carry out the vision for your congregation. An organized spiritual life can help you to do this on a regular basis.

Like Moses, you can go to God with all things.

An organized spiritual life starts with gathering regularly with other believers for worship. When we hear God's word read, preached, and sung, God can speak to our hearts and minds. Through broken bread and poured wine, Christ is present to forgive us, strengthen us, and heal us. As a congregational leader, commit yourself to regular worship attendance.

In addition, if you have not yet developed a habit of regular scripture reading and prayer, begin this as soon as possible. The discipline of personal time alone with God's word can give you increased insight and discernment. In regular prayer, you'll discover much-needed support and peace. Here are some suggestions for developing regular scripture reading and prayer in your life.

- *Chose a specific time, if possible.* Some people find that the best time for their daily quiet time is the first thing in the morning. The day's distractions can easily crowd out even the best intentions.

- *Chose a specific place, if possible.* This may take some creativity. It may be helpful to set aside a special chair or space in your home or to read scripture or pray as you wait in your car, ride the subway or bus, or go for a walk. Whatever you choose, seek to be consistent.

- *Gather the resources you need.* Choose a translation of the Bible and stick with it. You may find yourself underlining passages that speak to you, so have a pen or pencil ready.

Relax, read, reflect, pray.

- *Follow a simple outline:* relax, read, reflect, pray. If you can, take a few minutes to relax so you can focus on the moment. Read a passage of scripture, picking up where you left off the day before. Read until something in the text speaks to you. Reflect on what you've read, how and why it speaks to you, and the meaning it may have for the day. Conclude with prayer.

- *Read books on prayer or attend classes on prayer.* If your congregation doesn't offer classes on how to pray, consider offering one yourself or ask your pastor to help organize one.

- *Finally, don't give up!* Overwhelmed with fatigue, Moses called out to God and God answered. Before you decide that nothing can fix a particular problem, why not take it to God first? God has an amazing sense of humor and you may be surprised by the answer you get.

Chapter 3

Organizing for Hospitality

"I believe that I cannot by my own understanding or effort believe in Jesus Christ my Lord, or come to him. But the Holy Spirit has called me through the Gospel, enlightened me with his gifts, made me holy, and kept me in the true faith, just as he calls, gathers, enlightens, and sanctified and kept me in true faith."

—Martin Luther,
on the meaning of the Third Article of the Apostles' Creed,
The Small Catechism, copyright © Augsburg Fortress, Publishers

Organizing for hospitality begins with these questions: How might we inadvertently be hampering the efforts of the Spirit to call and gather the community? We may have a great desire to share the good news, but are we doing anything that sends people away? Is the space we create for newcomers a place of respite and hospitality or just empty seats? The Holy Spirit continues to call people to enter our churches. Some of these people are strangers, while others might have known us for ages. Have we done all we can to prepare a place for them?

In ancient Semitic culture, people believed that the surrounding desert was always more hostile to life than the stranger who might occasionally stroll in from it. The heat, lack of water, wild animals, and bandits threatened travelers. It became customary to welcome all travelers and strangers and offer them respite from their stressful trip. The exchange, however, wasn't always one-sided. Guests had stories to tell about places they had seen and unusual people they had encountered. Hearing about the experiences of others provided the hosts with new information and opened up a world previously unknown.

Welcoming guests in congregations

See "Keys to Hospitality" on pages 87-89 for practical sugges-tions on organizing for hospitality.

In congregations, welcoming a guest will change the host. Guests have stories to tell, and these stories help us discover the impact the gospel has had on their lives. We may even hear the subtle breath of the Holy Spirit who sent the guest in our direction. Guests may have specific needs, needs that we may come to understand as promptings of the Spirit. These guests are looking for something, maybe only respite from the heavy load they've been carrying in life. By listening to their needs, we can discern how the congregation can be open and inviting rather than a place to be avoided at all costs. Organizing for hospitality is not merely a set of programs. It's a matter of the heart and mind.

Working toward excellence

Look at the needs of your congre-gation's visitors and neighbors with the tool "Seeing Our Congregation Through New Eyes" on pages 90-92.

Listening to the needs of potential guests is the first step in organizing for hospitality. This means paying attention to the hurts and sense of brokenness that may send guests in the direction of the congregation. The community of faith must continue to remember the needs of its members and what is going on in the lives of those not yet part of the congregation. By doing so, the congregation begins the process of seeking excellence, of meeting the needs of others effectively and with quality.

In this context, *excellence* is defined as meeting the real needs of guests. This is markedly different than providing a menu of services and assuming that people will simply choose from what is already being offered. It suggests that a congregation has taken seriously the challenge of Matthew 25 and wishes to answer the question:

Lord, when was it that we saw you hungry and gave you food, or thirsty and gave you something to drink? And when was it that we saw you a stranger and welcomed you, or naked and gave you clothing? And when was it that we saw you sick or in prison and visited you?

—Matthew 25:37-39

People today are hungering for fellowship, fulfillment, meaning, and a connection with something beyond themselves.

It is in the best interest of every congregation—and it serves the proclamation of the gospel—to work toward excellence. The congregation should become a learning congregation, with each work group and planning team continually testing itself to determine whether its work is being accomplished effectively and, in response to external feedback, searching for ways to improve. This means answering the questions, addressing the needs, and appropriately responding to the stories guests bring to your congregation. This is the essence of organizing for hospitality.

For more information on listening to needs, see *Our Context: Exploring Our Congregation and Community.*

Serving people effectively

Many businesses and large nonprofit organizations have internalized Total Quality Management (TQM) programs. Although there are many approaches to such programs, the original version attempted in the 1980s and 1990s was based on material produced by W. Edwards Deming, an industrial engineer and physicist who consulted with Japanese industry in the early 1950s.

The congregation should become a learning congregation.

The church can learn from corporate management systems such as TQM, especially from the emphasis on listening to the people we are trying to reach. For our purposes, this means effectively serving people and measuring or evaluating the results to find areas for improvement.

Happy guests are returning guests

The congregation should focus its ministry on effectively serving people, rather than on meeting its own needs for institutional survival. The new mission field is across your street. If your council or planning team has not already done so, use the "Seeing Our Congregation Through New Eyes" tool to create a composite picture of people who live in the neighborhood but are not members of a

The new mission field is across your street.

community of faith. What are the demographics, work habits, belief systems, and so forth of these people? What are their expected needs? Are you currently organized to meet those needs?

Measurement and evaluation

**What worked
this time around?**

Some congregational leaders get caught up in the numbers game, believing that growth is the only possible evidence of faithfulness in ministry. Yet there are far more congregations in which leaders prefer not to look at data that might reveal new possibilities or uncomfortable truths.

If your council or planning team wants to improve the quality of your ministry, you must spend time reviewing both the good news and the bad news. The intent is to gather sufficient information so that future planners will know what worked and what didn't the next time the program or project is offered. At the end of your program, Sunday school year, or vacation Bible school, sit down with key leaders and ask, "What worked this time around?" Record this information. Then ask, "What specific areas need improvement?" This, too, is important information to record and save for next the next time. Volunteers may come and go in your congregation, so it is important to keep good records and let members of the staff and planning teams know where the records are kept. Don't depend on the long-term

---

If the number of visitors (as opposed to members) at worship services averages 10 people per month, members of an evangelism planning team might regularly look at these figures and think they are doing well.

But members of the planning team might not see that the average number of visitors has not changed in five years, while the church's membership declined slightly.

Or, the education team might regularly review the overall Sunday school enrollment, but rarely spend more than a few minutes trying to understand those findings.

memories of the planning team. Even if the same people are doing the planning next time around, they are likely to forget a detail that could make a tremendous difference in the outcome.

With the information properly recorded, the next planning group can make sure they provide the same level of service and quality. Once you have this assurance from one year to the next, choose one or two areas that needed improvement. Develop an action plan and take a different approach. You may need to pull together a new task force or project team to organize and implement the area targeted for improvement.

What specific areas need improvement?

Because participants come and go, it is important to continually evaluate the hits and misses in your ministry. Don't be surprised if something that made a splash last year receives only a yawn the next time around. The participants' needs will vary depending on who happens to attend, so focus on the changing needs of the current participants instead of saying, "We've always done it this way."

As you work through the evaluation of programs and projects, you may discover a ministry that has outlived its usefulness and needs to be dropped to free up resources for different approaches. This may cause confusion and grief in those who have a vested interest in maintaining that particular ministry. Think about all the people who will be affected by the change. These are usually called "stake holders" because they have a stake in what they created in the past and, depending on the change, may have a stake in the new. Be sure all stake holders involved in an old ministry and the new receive all the information possible and have an opportunity to be heard. Making changes without including everyone is usually counter-productive, even when the changes are based on good data from a planning and feedback process. Be as gentle and understanding as possible with those who aren't ready to release a ministry that is past its time.

You will not be able to look for areas in need of improvement unless you are willing to identify, analyze, and understand the problems. Notice, however, that the focus is on finding ways to improve the ministry, not on blaming individuals for failure.

The ultimate goal

In the business world, two questions guide much of what a successful company does: "What's your business?" and "How's business?" Businesses sometimes fail because they become more interested in defending themselves against charges of poor service than in figuring out what changes would bring back customers. Those companies that thrive understand the old rule: "Give customers what they want and can't get anywhere else."

How's business in the congregation?

As part of the church, we are in the "business" of conveying the good news. Our Lord set us loose with the great commission: "Go therefore and make disciples of all nations" (Matthew 28:19). How's business in the congregation? If our proclamation is objectively sound but subjectively uninspiring and irrelevant to people's needs, if we have all the right answers to questions no one is asking, or if people are not satisfied with our ministry, they may never hear the good news that God has set them free in Jesus Christ.

Every part of the congregation's work should center on this ultimate goal.

It is possible, of course, for people to be satisfied with the congregation's ministry yet still feel unchallenged, uninformed, and unmotivated. This, of course, is not the best way to meet people's needs. Instead, your congregation can serve people effectively and evaluate results so that participants are eager and pleased about programs or events, new members get involved and then get even more involved, and people find strength for living and hope for the future through your ministry.

Reflect on the goals of your congregation and the council and planning teams. Do your goals make sense in light of the perceived needs of the people you are trying to reach? Do you regularly evaluate your goals by asking people what effect the work of the congregation has had on their lives? Many congregations tend to focus on themselves instead of their service. Every part of the congregation's work should center on this ultimate goal: enabling people to find a deeper relationship with Jesus Christ and to live their lives as his disciples.

Chapter 4

Selecting and Recruiting Volunteers

Now there are varieties of gifts, but the same Spirit; and there are varieties of service, but the same Lord; and there are varieties of activities, but it is the same Lord who activates all of them in everyone. To each is given the manifestation of the Spirit for the common good.

—1 Corinthians 12:4-7

A story about involvement

"We have to get them involved!" George said. as he was enjoying the lunch conversation with several other pastors from his area. "Our most active members are the ones who've gotten involved in the ministries of the congregation. They feel connected, they hang in there with us longer, and they make things happen. They're also our best givers."

"Yeah, well, at least your people are willing to serve in some way," Audrey said. "No matter what we do, we keep hearing, 'I'm too busy,' 'I'm burned out from the last time I got involved,' or 'Try me again next year.' I'm stuck and out of ideas."

Late in the conversation, Ellen added, "I have a different set of problems. There are two people who seem to dominate whatever group they join. When other people find out that either one of these two people will be part of a ministry or project, they want nothing to do with it. Because there are so few people left who will volunteer, these two are starting to run everything. Now nothing new can happen."

Maintaining structure to fulfilling mission

Some congregations seem to have all the volunteers they need, and their ministries function smoothly and efficiently. Joy permeates nearly everything they do and their vision is contagious. You can't help but feel the mutual support when you spend time with the members. At the same time, other congregations are mired in endless meetings that produce burned-out volunteers who question the value of offering their gifts of time and talent. How does a congregation move from bumping along in frustration to engaging its members in fulfilling mission and ministry?

Our world has changed over the last several decades, and these changes have affected the church. People are less willing to make commitments, those who are employed may have different shifts or longer commutes, and changing expectations of the church have made a real impact on the way congregations and their members function. On the other hand, these very changes have opened up tremendous opportunities. Many people today are hungry for fellowship, authentic community, and a place to belong, and they are willing to give up other things for this. The Holy Spirit continues to call and gather together the body of Christ.

How a congregation organizes its ministries will show if it is mission-oriented or working merely to meet the needs of the institution. This can also be seen in the roles and tasks given to individuals.

As you consider how to best carry out the vision in your congregation, remember that people aren't simply looking to serve on planning teams. Rather, they are looking for opportunities to use their gifts in ways that are deeply fulfilling.

Most people today have overloaded schedules, but they will find ways to block out time for what's important to them.

A mission-oriented congregation will serve the emotional and spiritual needs of individual members and the community. The primary goal will be to help people grow as disciples as they are equipped to reach into the surrounding community as "little Christs."

Identifying potential volunteers

Think carefully about who might like to participate in your congregation's ongoing mission and ministry. This is not to suggest that a congregation can ignore basic things that need to be done and simply focus on the individual needs of volunteers. That would produce chaos! Developing organizational structure involves identifying and grouping the work that needs to be performed so it can be delegated to people who are in the congregation. But carrying out the vision is more than defining tasks that have to be accomplished. The work of the congregation will happen with joy and excitement when the passions and gifts of members are included in the organizing process.

You are in a position to help potential volunteers discover how their time and abilities are part of their stewardship of God's gifts. Discover what motivates individuals to get involved and then encourage them to use their time and talents in ways that are appropriate to them. When you invite people to participate in the ministry of your congregation, you need to consider gifts, skills, availability, inclusiveness, and age.

Gifts

The apostle Paul writes that spiritual gifts are given to persons for the specific purpose of building up the body of Christ: "To each is given the manifestation of the Spirit for the common good" (1 Corinthians 12:7). There are attitudes and personality traits that tear down a congregation rather than build it up, but Paul aimed to help Christians to be effective in proclaiming the good news by using their gifts and passions in positive ways.

Called to Lead: A Handbook for Lay Leaders also discusses selecting and recruiting volunteers.

Consider gifts, skills, availability, inclusiveness, and age.

Everyone has at least one spiritual gift that can assist the congregation.

Everyone has at least one spiritual gift that can assist the congregation. If you have not yet done so, consider adding a spiritual gift inventory to your process of involving new members. From the very beginning, new members will know you are serious about helping them grow and mature spiritually. This is also the first step in understanding what gifts newcomers bring into the congregation.

Paul identified many spiritual gifts. In Romans 12:6-8, Paul mentions prophecy, ministry, teaching, exhortation, giving, leadership, and compassion. In 1 Corinthians 12:8-11, the list of spiritual gifts includes wisdom, knowledge, faith, healing, prophecy, discernment, and interpretation. Galatians 5:22-23 says "the fruit of the Spirit is love, joy, peace, patience, kindness, generosity, faithfulness, gentleness, and self-control."

Even more spiritual gifts can be identified. For example, some people have the gift of leadership, while others have gifts to support those leaders and carry out the vision. Some people are gifted in seeing future possibilities. Others have gifts to take those dreams and forge them into specific, manageable goals. Still others have gifts to turn those goals into action plans that can be embraced by individuals or groups. Some people have the ability to work independently, while others gain the greatest satisfaction from being part of a group. Some people are able to juggle multiple tasks, while others prefer to focus on one thing at a time. Some people are best at beginning with small details and expanding to the larger project. Others are just the opposite—they live to take on large, complex issues and break them down into smaller pieces.

Does your congregation provide opportunities to volunteers for growth and training in using their gifts? Opportunities to receive training can give confidence to volunteers and make it more likely that they will say yes in the future. Before someone becomes a greeter at a worship service, does the congregation provide training on how to extend hospitality? Before someone reads a lesson during worship, has anyone helped him or her with tips on reading publicly and deciphering the occasional Old Testament name that looks unpronounceable?

No matter what the training, at times you will find that someone is frustrated and doesn't get any satisfaction out of a task. The ministry may slow to a crawl and recipients of the individual's efforts may feel they've been missing out on something. This might mean that the person is trying to do something that's not in an area of his or her strongest gifts. Not everyone who volunteers will serve effectively. When necessary, leaders must be able to diplomatically release people to serve in other ways in the congregation.

Skills

To help members of your congregation give of themselves in the most satisfying way, you also need to take into account the skills they have acquired. Most skills are gathered through practice, but they can also be developed through formal education, on-the-job training, or long-term experience. Everyone from barbers to nurses to pilots receive instruction and supervision while learning the work. Some skills, such as carpentry, traditionally have developed under the eye of an experienced mentor.

Many congregations keep careful records that include the occupations, hobbies, and interests of their members. For members who are employed, it is helpful to include some description of actual work responsibilities, in addition to job titles or categories.

Other skills are not immediately obvious, but often are even more important in a congregation's life together. Life experiences, such as dealing with suffering or tragedy, or successfully negotiating the joys and pitfalls of aging, leave their indelible mark in someone's heart and mind. Individuals who have sought to understand life experiences in light of the healing power of the gospel may have a spiritual maturity that is important when you seek Sunday school teachers, leaders, mentors for confirmation students, or anyone else involved in helping others grow as disciples of Jesus Christ.

Not everyone will want to carry their work life over into the life of the congregation. A bank manager may be unwilling to serve on the finance planning team because she would like to use other skills.

Perhaps she wants to develop a shelter program for people who are homeless or teach hospitality skills to ushers and greeters. In addition, don't assume people will donate skills that they usually are paid to use. A plumber in your congregation, for example, might choose to decline the usual fee for helping to unclog a drain, but don't expect the plumber to do work for free simply because he or she is a member of your church.

Availability

Be realistic in your expectations.

In addition to gifts and skills, you will also need to consider availability when you invite people to participate in the ministry of the congregation. In some situations, people are excluded from participation because of factors they may not mention, even though they may have the needed skills, gifts, and interests. Members might be unable to meet at certain times due to work schedules and commuting times, the availability of child care, and the amount of time it will takes them to get to and from a meeting. Make sure the sidewalks and parking lots around your church building or other meeting location are well-lit at night, free of obstacles, and clear of snow and ice.

Be realistic in your expectations. The members of your congregation have a variety of interests, commitments, and struggles. They may be involved with work, family and friends, children's activities, hobbies, continuing education, or recreational activities. In addition, they may have more than one job, be struggling to make ends meet, or dealing with unemployment, health problems, disabilities, and other issues.

Inclusiveness

The Evangelical Lutheran Church in America (ELCA) has adopted an operating principle called "inclusiveness," which means striving to reflect the diversity of a congregation when people are selected to serve in our ministries. An obvious place to begin is with gender and ethnicity. Whether or not your congregation's constitution calls for it, the leaders of your congregation should give attention to inclusiveness when selecting volunteers. All people are created and loved by God. In Christ, and in his body the church, all human distinctions are superseded. The unique gifts of each person are needed to build up the whole church.

Gender equality usually will be easier to attain since most congregations have significant numbers of both men and women. Avoid making assumptions based on stereotypes. Women will not automatically prefer the education planning team over the property planning team. Men might find more personal fulfillment on the worship and music committee than on the finance committee.

Dealing with multicultural possibilities might be more challenging for your congregation. For example, although the vast majority of ELCA members are of northern European ancestry, the ELCA as a whole is working to expand its numbers of African American, Asian, Latino, Arab and Middle Eastern, Native American, and Alaska Native members. Your congregation might make deliberate efforts to reach out to people from one or more ethnic communities. If so, you will also want to involve members from these communities in the planning teams and ministry of your congregation.

Age

Age is another factor to consider as you think about the pool of people who can be asked to serve in your congregation's ministries. Although many people do not fit these life stage descriptions exactly, knowing general developmental characteristics can help you anticipate the needs and gifts of the members of your congregation.

Adolescence

Adolescence is the time of transition from childhood to adulthood. At this stage of life, young people take more responsibility and begin to function independently from their parents. Young people may be interested in their congregation, and this is a good time to help them

The unique gifts of each person are needed to build up the whole church.

become involved in planning and carrying out ministries that benefit others. Adolescents will often respond well when invited to put their faith into action.

The 20s

Your task is to invite them to a living faith in Jesus Christ.

The decade of the 20s is the time when people usually establish their adult identities. They may continue their education, start careers, or search for committed adult friendships and relationships. This often is a time when individuals leave groups or institutions that were significant earlier in life. In their faith lives, people in their 20s may be at a point where they move beyond childhood beliefs to a mature, grounded faith in Christ.

People in the United States who are now in their 20s are less likely than previous generations to have had experience with the church during childhood. People in this generation may have limited knowledge of biblical stories, denominational differences, and how a congregation operates. Everything that congregations have understood will be challenged by the rising number of people who have no experience with the church.

Rather than inviting people in this age group to be involved in something they've known (the church), your task is to invite them to a living faith in Jesus Christ. If planning teams and other working groups in your congregation can find ways to help people in their 20s with important life tasks, some will become willing and enthusiastic partners in mission. These partners will bring the energy and understanding of their generation that will be critical for a congregation's healthy mission-oriented future.

The 30s

The decade of the 30s is a time when people may dedicate themselves to accomplishments and careers and perhaps to raising a family. To some extent, the achievements of people in their 30s may distract them from volunteering their time for work in a congregation, but they may be interested in things that have a direct bearing on their

The baby boom generation, now in the 40s and 50s, has consistently sought to forge ahead into the future on their own terms and change the rules for what is expected of them.

Baby boomers may not volunteer time and talents in the same fashion as previous generations. They may look to do only things that are meaningful to them. As a result, their attitudes about volunteerism may clash with other generations.

They also may look for volunteer commitments that have shorter time frames and use more of their intellectual and experiential gifts.

lives. They may participate more readily in short-term projects or those that don't demand a great deal of time.

The 40s

When people reach their 40s, they tend to assess how life has gone so far. Some decide to make changes, such as beginning a new career or finding new ways to achieve personal satisfaction. Still others focus on the years ahead, especially if health has become an issue. All in all, this may be an introspective decade. People at this stage of their life can be extremely valuable to your ministries, with the skills and experience they have accumulated. They may be inclined to ask, "Why?" and therefore can focus on questions of purpose and direction for your congregation.

The 50s

The 50s often is a period of integration. People at this point may have completed the life review begun in the 40s, and changes may have been made as a result. These people may have already attained or revised their career goals. They also may be dealing with problems such as age discrimination or the need to care for aged parents or grandchildren. People in their 50s can also be very interested in learning new things and may be among your most willing and productive volunteers.

The 60s

 People in their 60s may make a transition from working for pay to retiring. Some continue to work for financial reasons, especially if they can't meet expenses with Social Security, have no pension, or are raising grandchildren. These people may be willing and productive volunteers and some might have more time than ever to give of themselves for the good of your congregation's mission and ministries.

The 70s

The most significant factor for people in their 70s may be health, but this is also a time when many people are most able and willing to give of themselves. As you think about the contributions people in this group can make, you need to take into account factors such as their degree of mobility and general health. Do they need transportation? Does one person begin avoiding evening meetings because of security concerns or poor night vision? Does another avoid writing, sitting for prolonged periods, or walking because of arthritis?

The 80s and above

People in their 80s and above may continue to serve as their health allows, and they may be mainstays of prayer chains and caring ministries such as maintaining telephone contacts with homebound members. One of the most valuable roles they might play is to provide counsel and advice to younger leaders or to serve as mentors to confirmation students and other young people. People age 80 and above can be personal witnesses to the faith that sustains them and to the impact of the congregation on their lives.

Length of service

When we agree to take on a task, most of us like to know not only what is involved, but also when we start working and how we will know the task is finished. These things are fairly easy for a task force or project team to determine because they are formed for a specific purpose. Planning teams or committees, on the other hand, are usually described in more general terms.

Terms of office

When it comes time to recruit members for a planning team, you might identify the start and finish of a term of office. Although a one-year term works best in some settings, a two-year term allows more time for orienting new members, planning, and completing some work before the group's membership changes again. When terms are only a year long, a working group might change entirely each year. If possible, establish a rotation system so that some current members remain to provide continuity even as others are bringing new ideas and new perspectives to the tasks at hand.

In some congregations there is a limit to how many consecutive terms a person can serve. This provides some protection for the individual because without a limit a person might feel pressured to stay on with a working group long after he or she has lost energy or interest. Term limits provide some protection for the congregation as well, by ensuring that there will be new energy and fresh ideas in working groups and ministries, and opening up possibilities for newer members to make a contribution.

There can and should be many partners who help select and recruit people to serve.

Coordinating recruitment

There can and should be many partners who help select and recruit people to serve in the ministries and working groups of your congregation. These include:

- *The Nominating Committee.* This group can help align the gifts and talents of members with the needs of the various planning teams or committees.

- *The Stewardship Committee.* Part of the work of this committee is to to devise ways to help people offer time and talents to the congregation and providing for record keeping and follow-up with those who offer to serve.

Coordination is needed so those responsible for recruiting others aren't calling the same people.

- *The Coordinator of Volunteers.* This person may be part of the paid staff and usually is responsible for maintaining up-to-date information about the interests people have expressed, where their gifts and passions might be, and who currently is serving in what capacities. A volunteer coordinator may also be responsible for logistics, such as sending out meeting notices and distributing minutes.

- *The Pastor(s) and staff members.* In many cases the pastor and staff members will have the most complete information about the gifts, skills, abilities, and availability of the members of the congregation. Their suggestions can be especially helpful when leaders are looking for ways to involve new members or those who have not had much previous involvement.

- *The Congregation Council.* In the *Model Constitution for Congregations of the ELCA*, the duties of the congregation council include "to seek to involve all members of this congregation in worship, learning, witness, service, and support" (C12.04.b). The council might fulfill this duty by regularly reviewing the structure of working groups to determine whether they are operating effectively and by suggesting names of people who have the potential to fill leadership roles in the congregation.

As you consider inviting people to participate in your congregation's mission and ministry, remember that coordination is needed so those responsible for recruiting others aren't calling the same people. This could be the responsibility of a coordinator of volunteers, the pastor(s), the stewardship planning team, or the congregation council. The individual or group in charge of coordinating would receive requests for volunteers from all the planning teams, task forces, and other ministries. In most congregations, it would be unrealistic to expect one person or group to do all the actual recruiting for the congregation's needs. If those responsible for coordinating recruitment maintain a good database and make available a list of people who seem to fit particular needs, leaders of the working groups can contact individuals on the list directly. The individual or group in charge of recruitment could also work closely with the spiritual gifts inventory for the congregation, using information from the inventory to help newcomers quickly find a niche in the congregation.

Some congregations have found it helpful to contact all their members on a regular basis with a very specific list of the volunteer help that will be needed during upcoming months. This does not restrict recruiting only to those who volunteer, but provides a good starting point. Other methods are to place a detailed list of needs for help in each week's bulletin or newsletter or invite people to offer their gifts and time along with their financial resources when the offering is received in worship.

Whatever system you use to invite people to volunteer, follow up on offers to help. Also, be aware that not everyone who is able and willing to serve will want to volunteer in this way. Leaders must also identify and recruit gifted people through other means.

Follow up on offers to help.

Effective invitations

When you are inviting an individual or group to take on a task, a personal visit, conversation in the hallway, or phone call is far more effective than placing an article in the newsletter. In this instance, it usually is best for a leader or group to select and recruit individuals in order to achieve inclusiveness and a mix of gifts, skills, and availability. The most effective recruitment will match the gifts of individuals with the needs of the congregation and its ministry. This opens doors to volunteer opportunities that are rewarding and fulfilling.

Chapter 5

Communicating for Understanding and Acceptance

Then [Jesus] took the twelve aside and said, 'See, we are going up to Jerusalem, and everything that is written about the Son of Man by the prophets will be accomplished. For he will be handed over to the Gentiles; and he will be mocked and insulted and spat upon. After they have flogged him, they will kill him, and on the third day he will rise again.' But they understood nothing about all these things; in fact, what he said was hidden from them, and they did not grasp what was said.

—Luke 18:31-34

Understanding and acceptance are two key components of the communication process.

For the third time in Luke's Gospel, Jesus tries to tell the disciples what awaits him at the end of their journey. And for the third time, the disciples display their incomprehension. They don't get it. They don't understand the sounds of tomorrow's beckoning. Because they don't understand, they can't accept what is about to happen. On the night Jesus is arrested, they flee into the darkness, and Peter denies Jesus three times. The next day, only a handful of followers are present at the crucifixion. Not understanding the reason for the journey to Jerusalem, the disciples are incapable of accepting its meaning.

It's true that even if they had understood Jesus' words, the disciples might not have accepted the outcome. In this case, the disciples' lack of understanding directly impacts their ability to accept what happens. Whether it was preconceived notions or a limited ability to think beyond their own understandings of the world, they couldn't hear what Jesus was trying to tell them. As a result, the unfolding of events caught them off-guard. This caused them to react emotionally, and most of them ran away. Only after the resurrection would the early Christian community remember Jesus' words about going to Jerusalem and fully grasp their meaning.

Understanding and acceptance

Understanding and acceptance are two key components of the communication process. Understanding happens when we know the situation or can grasp what needs to be done. It's the "I hear what you want and I know where you're coming from" moment in working together. Acceptance means we have heard the vision, understand the necessity of going along with the idea, and are ready to take action. The work ahead is now part of us and we're ready to get busy. For understanding and acceptance to occur, good communication must happen in both directions, completely involving the people on both sides of the interaction, those wishing to give away a task or authority and those people willing and ready to accept that responsibility or authority.

If you have not already come to this discovery on your own, you will find that unless understanding and acceptance occur between individuals, varying levels of confusion result. This bewilderment often causes frustration, which can lead to anger or fear. Failure to reach mutual understanding and acceptance before giving away or accepting a responsibility is the root cause of many congregational

See "The Burning Bush" on page 93 to see how God and Moses reached understanding and acceptance.

Called to Lead: A Handbook for Lay Leaders also discusses communication in small groups or planning teams.

Obtaining understanding and obtaining acceptance are two separate actions. Understanding must always be obtained first. Without mutual understanding, acceptance of a task, job or project will be based on false assumptions, leaving behind negative feelings and unmet responsibilities.

conflicts. Good communication is the key to preventing this from happening in your planning teams and other working groups.

Hints for gaining understanding

- Make sure you understand what the group is trying to accomplish.

- Get people involved early in the planning process so that they have fundamental knowledge of the goals and resulting action plans.

- Make sure the steps make sense and ask for feedback along the way. Have members of the group explain the project to you. (Explaining it to you will ensure they understand it themselves.)

- Give people time to think about a task before they take on responsibility for carrying it out. Someone who agrees to take on a task does not necessarily understand what needs to be done. Try not to make unwarranted assumptions that people new to a working group will know how things have been done in the past. One approach is to discuss the objective and the procedures previously used by the group, and then to ask the person to reflect on this a while and see if he or she can come up with a better way of doing things. Or, you can ask people to get back to you at a later date, giving them time to further study what's required of them.

- Continually bring up the importance of understanding and acceptance. Before the end of a planning meeting, brief interaction, or e-mail exchange, remind everyone that understanding and acceptance are of utmost importance before carrying out any task.

Hints for gaining acceptance

- Keep in mind that gaining acceptance is another way of describing commitment. Commitment means that someone has decided to risk getting involved by setting aside time for you and the ministry that's been assigned.

- Don't coerce, badger, or annoy someone into taking on a task. No one, particularly a volunteer, will accept a task if pushed into it. If pushed hard enough, individuals will give up, cut back on their involvement, or leave entirely.

- Ask people to accept tasks that are suited to their particular spiritual gifts or passions. If tasks don't fit their gifts or if they do something only because they think they should, people will eventually feel emotionally disconnected from the project at hand and, ultimately, not responsible for the outcome.

No one, particularly a volunteer, will accept a task if pushed into it.

Making sure your message is getting through

The ability to communicate well with others goes a long way in building trust, which leads to positive relationships. If there isn't a positive relationship between a leader and the rest of the planning team or working group, little may be accomplished.

In today's society, we've learned well the lessons of division and rancor. We're not nearly so good at forming and maintaining trusting relationships, finding consensus, handling situations that involve opposing viewpoints, or finding ways to speak to and hear persons who come from different places than ourselves. It's easiest to learn these skills in a trusting environment where they can be practiced. Congregations can promote this kind of environment by providing opportunities for education and transformation amid the actual work that is being done. If a class on basic communication and listening skills is not already regularly offered in your congregation, consider starting one. Such a class could be set up as an adult education forum or part of leadership training or an ongoing household or parent enrichment program. As individuals learn to speak and listen effectively, the expertise they gain will pay off in all the nooks and crannies of their lives, including the organizational structures of your congregation.

Effective feedback

At Incarnation, the evangelism planning team received no information about their responsibilities beyond "Help bring people to church." The team, understanding that to mean they had permission to define the task themselves, accepted the challenge and set to work. They carried out what they believed to be effective ways to welcome people with no church homes into their congregation. Later, team members became disappointed and angry when word got back to them that others in the congregation were dissatisfied with what they had been doing.

How can you avoid this kind of unfortunate breakdown in communication?

Others didn't approve of who was now joining the congregation: "These are strangers, they're not like us at all." The evangelism team reacted defensively: "But they're God's children just like us. Isn't that the point, to go and make disciples of all nations?"

How can you avoid this kind of unfortunate breakdown in communication, which destroys enthusiasm for the work of the congregation? The confusion might have been avoided if there had been understanding and acceptance from the very beginning. The answer at this point rests in a setting up a feedback process to ensure that everyone involved in a ministry is communicated with directly, reopen doors of conversation, lower the anxiety level, and allow you to get back to the original assignment.

Suggestions for sharing effective feedback

- Always use the pronoun "I" when communicating. Starting a conversation with "You" immediately puts the other person on the defensive. "I noticed the number of return visitors has gone down slightly" is a much better way of entering the conversation than "Why are you doing this?" Also, it's always better to speak for yourself, to convey what you actually know, rather than sharing, "I've heard people talk" or "Some people are saying." Avoid speaking for others unless you have collected information from them as part of your desire to understand what's going on.

- Begin by sharing the information you know. For example: "In the last six months we have had 40 percent of our visitors return. In the six months prior to that, 60 percent of our visitors returned." Starting your feedback with actual facts and quantifiable information allows communication to focus on the results and not the person. This will set the stage for you to focus on the process that might need improvement or the project's goals and action plan. Focus on the problem and the information, but not on the personalities.

- Share your interpretations of what you think the information might mean. "I'm thinking the decline in return of visitors is related to our current follow-up process. But I'm also wondering if there's anything we've changed in worship that is having less appeal." Base your interpretation on what you actually know, and make it clear that you are looking for solutions and not trying to lay blame.

- After sharing your interpretations, you may describe how you feel about the situation. "This is what I think the information is telling us, and I feel sad about it. The neighborhood is changing and I've noticed that most of the visitors who aren't returning are Asian. I'm disappointed that they might not feel welcomed here."

- After sharing information, interpretations, and feelings, ask what the other person thinks and feels about the situation. Give that individual, or the entire team, the opportunity to do this. Again, the task is to mutually find a solution that helps you reach your original goal, not to fault the group for their work.

- Ask five *why* questions. Use a piece of newsprint and start with, "Why isn't this working?" From the answers given, ask a *why* question based on the new information, such as "Why don't Asian visitors feel comfortable worshiping here?" By continuing to ask "Why?" eventually you will get to the root cause and a place to restart your planning.

Focus on the problem, the information, and not on the personalities.

Becoming a team

Effective teams have a shared understanding of their authority and have accepted the responsibility delegated to them. (Chapter 6 covers authority and delegated responsibility in more detail.) They also need to know how to function as a team. This requires that team members be people-oriented as well as task-oriented. The two are not mutually exclusive. In general, the groups that most successfully accomplish their tasks are those that attend to the relationships within the group and the needs of others as they work together.

A team has to be built.

Each person on a well-functioning team adds to and complements the strengths of others. The team can compensate for individual limitations and support individual gifts. But a team doesn't just fall into place and immediately start its work. A team has to be built.

Groups progress through three steps as they become a team: forming, storming, and norming.

Forming

Every time a new group comes together, individuals need to get acquainted with one another. This step should not be bypassed in order to begin dealing with the work of the group. Let members of a new group spend some time getting to know one another by sharing some of their history, their experiences, and hopes for the group. It may be helpful to start each meeting with a check-in time, time set aside for members to share the high and low points in their lives since the last time the group was together.

Storming

In the storming phase, friction develops because individuals have different personalities, dreams, expectations, and understandings of the task of the group. If behavior is not abrasive or abusive, some degree of friction is not necessarily a problem. Discussion at this point can help individuals in the group to come to a mutual understanding of their assignment so that members of the group can then accept the group responsibility they share as well as their individual responsibilities.

Norming

The next and continuing phase is norming. This is the ideal situation, a group has come together as a team and is ready to expend mutual effort. In addition, if the team is to be successful, members will adjust to changing conditions and the actions of other individuals on the team. It takes time for team members to learn to make these adjustments smoothly.

Although team members might not form friendships while they work, they should be collegial and respectful of one another. Being respectful includes, among other things, taking into account the diversity present even in a small group. Rarely is there just one way to go about a task. Individuals have different personality types and approach any task with different working styles shaped by their background and culture.

An effective team leader or chair can contribute a lot to the group's work by displaying sensitivity to different working styles and to the way people relate to one another. Some people get off track easily, and the leader will need to bring the discussion back to the business at hand. Some people rub others the wrong way, and the leader may need to facilitate discussion by restating their contributions in a more positive and helpful way. Some team members will talk too much and others not enough, but the effective leader will steer discussions so that all members have an opportunity to make contributions.

Learn more about growing through conflict with *Our Community: Dealing with Conflict in Our Congregation.*

Conflict

Where there is no conflict, there is no life. Congregational groups are not exempt from communication problems and conflict. At some point, most groups will deal with conflict over facts and their interpretation, theological issues, ways to carry out the group's work, how to reach a goal, or differences in personalities. Some of these conflicts are healthy and can lead to learning and growth. We are forgiven saints and children of God, but also sinners who constantly fail to live up to our potential and identity. Be forgiving. Be charitable, and be prepared to continue working on interpersonal relationships and team building.

Chapter 6

Boundaries: Responsibility, Authority, and Accountability

And Jesus came and said to them, "All authority in heaven and on earth has been given to me. Go therefore and make disciples of all nations, baptizing them in the name of the Father and of the Son and of the Holy Spirit, and teaching them to obey everything that I have commanded you. And remember, I am with you always, to the end of the age."

—Matthew 28:18-20

One hot Saturday afternoon, my family and I were sitting by a pool. Out of nowhere, a golden Labrador retriever came sailing over a fence. Completely oblivious to our presence, in one graceful bound the dog splashed down in the pool. After two quick laps, she must have figured out we were there because she then trotted over and shook herself dry all over us. I called her owners, who came right over and led the dog home.

The value of boundaries

We were entertained by the golden retriever's unannounced flight across the fence line but things might have been different if young children had been playing where the dog landed. The fence was in place to regulate situations like this.

Boundaries in an organization make for better teams because they cause the interactions of people to be more predictable. In a planning team, these boundaries are built on responsibility, authority, and

**Boundaries
are built on
responsibility,
authority, and
accountability.**

accountability. Understanding these three components will give you the skills you need to set up appropriate boundaries for your planning team. These boundaries should not become a permanent wall between your team and other groups in the congregation or lock individuals into responsibilities that never change, but provide parameters within which mission and ministry will best function. With appropriate boundaries, planning teams and working groups will form and disband depending on the needs being addressed. Depending on what the team is attempting to accomplish at the time, individuals will take on different responsibilities and levels of authority and be held accountable.

Responsibility

Before accepting or assigning responsibility, everyone involved should understand the scope of the responsibility. It is vital that all parties know which type of responsibility is being put forth: responsibility for completion, responsibility for input or advice, or responsibility for service.

Responsibility for completion

With responsibility for completion, a planning team or an individual is responsible for the completion of the given or assigned task. Those with responsibility for completion are the ones publicly thanked when things go well. Assigning this level of responsibility helps draw a healthy boundary. Other groups or individuals may stand at the edge of this fence, but they don't have the right to climb over it unless they have been invited in. This is the highest level of responsibility that can be appropriately given in a congregation.

Responsibility for input or advice

Responsibility for input or advice gives a team or individual the responsibility to provide information and opinions to the group or individual with the responsibility of completion. When teams or individuals receive the responsibility to provide input or advice, they should also have the authority to be heard and taken seriously when the time comes.

Responsibility for service

Those who have responsibility for service are expected to fulfill the obligations assigned. This is best understood as direct service responsibility. For example, a keyboard player may have the responsibility of playing on Sunday morning and will be held accountable if she oversleeps. The administrative assistant may have the responsibility of copying the worship bulletin or newsletter when it is ready. Key lay people or staff members hired for a specific task often carry out direct service responsibilities.

Assign responsibility to positions rather than persons

Responsibilities should be assigned to positions (which are filled by people) but not to the specific people themselves. In smaller or less formal congregations, people may take on tasks based on their personal interests and talents, as long as no one else seems to want the job: "Sam always knows where to get the cheapest light bulbs, so he's a natural to change them in the sanctuary."

Over the long run, however, this can create a situation where the work done is more a reflection of the people's personal preferences than what needs to be done for the sake of the congregation. Further, in this scenario, every time a new person steps forward to volunteer for a job, the content, emphasis, and quality of the work also changes.

As the congregation grows or its ministries become more complex, making sure the needed work is actually done also grows in importance. The congregation can no longer wait for Sam to get back from vacation. The bulbs need to be replaced now, not when a particular person can get around to it.

With a well-defined job description for the task that needs to be accomplished, a series of dedicated people can move in and out of the job of lightbulb-changer with little adjustment to the basic responsibilities of the position. Responsibility can then be assigned and accepted based on a description of the tasks, not given away to a person in the hope that he or she will know what to do and will always be available when needed.

When a series of people can take on a task based on a job description, completion of the task doesn't depend on one person, and the congregation is better prepared to deal with individuals who tend to control and dominate rather than function as members of a team.

Authority

Sufficient authority must be provided to carry out the work and complete the task.

Simply assigning responsibility isn't enough. Sufficient authority must be provided to carry out the work and complete the task. When it comes to congregational life and the energy of volunteers, one thing is certain: people will not do much unless they can make decisions related to their passions and interests.

One of the dilemmas for congregations is how to maintain a sense of direction as a whole while allowing individuals to make some decisions in accomplishing their tasks. For example, imagine the motivation left over after a volunteer must wait for the next meeting of the building team before switching to a different brand of light bulbs. Perhaps that team must make a presentation to the congregation council and ask the treasurer to run a cost benefit analysis depending on energy usage, and then the treasurer must ask an electrical engineer what she thinks, and so on. The more authority and responsibility individuals or teams can exercise with respect to their tasks, the more likely the individual or team is to accomplish the task. This is a central principle in effective organization. Decisions and actions can happen more quickly, and there is less overall frustration when people have the authority they need to carry out their responsibilities. More is likely to be done well and in a timely fashion when sufficient authority is linked with an assigned responsibility. In this sense, authority and responsibility are closely related.

Confusion and conflict erupt when people have different views on who is *allowed* to do what. Authority is especially important during times of pastoral or staffing turnover or other major changes. Two types of authority can be assigned: informal authority and formal authority.

Informal authority

Many decisions in a congregation don't require multiple layers of structure. People who have the knowledge or experience are sought out to guide a particular part of the congregation's ministry. Perhaps one individual has great abilities in constructing a congregational budget. With informal authority, how that person goes about putting the budget together will become the way it's done—without regard to whether it's the best or most efficient way of accomplishing the task.

Informal authority is unwritten, undefined, and held by individuals, not assigned to a position. There is no formal job description other than the fact that the individual has always gone about the task in the same way. After doing an excellent job over the years, trust and leadership for a certain task falls to one individual who keeps on doing the work the way he or she has done it before.

Informal authority is unwritten, undefined, and held by individuals.

The drawback to this system is that informal authority has the potential to create great misunderstandings. New members wishing to become involved may jump into action in an area long occupied by a particular person. Not knowing there are unwritten rules for how to accomplish a certain task, they may offer up their time and talent in new and creative ways only to be told out of the blue, "That's Mary's job and she knows what she's doing." The information is usually not conveyed this directly, however, which only adds to the confusion.

Formal authority

Formal authority is usually defined, often in writing, and tends to be assigned (such as the assigned authority of the pastor or the congregation council). Formal authority is stable, known by all,

Formal authority is stable, known by all, and changes only with clear notice.

and changes only with clear notice. Because formal authority is assigned to a position, any person who occupies that position automatically assumes that authority. The congregation council president has certain authorities that are spelled out in a congregation's constitution. The pastor has certain authorities that can be spelled out in a letter of call or written down as part of the formal minutes of an annual or congregational meeting.

For some people, this may seem like part of the problem with congregational life—overly defined roles to the point where no creativity can spark up. Indeed, in a declining congregation this is exactly what happens. The roles of the council, pastor, and planning teams can become so thoroughly defined that they lock the congregation into its current position, making sure it can't move in any direction except to totter downward! As much as possible, define in writing what authority a position, team, working group, or council has in light of the vision, goals, and plans of the congregation. This can help to clear up confusion over such matters as who supervises the paid staff, who oversees financial matters, who manages the master church calendar, and who decides what outside groups can meet in the church building.

Accountability

Although individuals and teams should have as much responsibility and authority as needed to complete a task, they aren't given complete freedom. A congregation, planning team, or individual cannot work effectively if everyone does only whatever he or she wants. We need to work together to maximize the talents and gifts of individuals in the congregation. People generally are willing to give up some of their personal freedom when they are convinced that the work of the group is significant and that together the team will produce more than any one individual could achieve. Accountability ensures that everyone involved can participate at his or her fullest potential within understood and accepted limits.

Reporting relationships

A planning team, work group or individual is accountable to the congregation through the person or group that made the original appointment. If the congregation council appointed your planning team, the council has the right to evaluate the team's work. If your working group was appointed by the pastor or by a congregation council member who has responsibility for a specific ministry area, then that is the person to whom your group reports.

The leader who appoints or recruits someone to accomplish a task *delegates* responsibility for the task. The ability to delegate is a key leadership skill. When you delegate, you should also set up a way to obtain progress reports as the task is being carried out and an evaluation when it is completed. Establishing clear reporting relationships is one way to honor people's time, gifts, and other commitments. It is a sign of respect to be clear about what is expected and what is not.

Some people think that congregations do not need to be overly concerned with issues of accountability. They believe the church is like a family, and they reason that families don't function by a rulebook but on principles of love and support. On the other hand, although families are places of love and support, they also have many unwritten ways of behaving that become standards for what is acceptable and what isn't. Smaller congregations are, indeed, more like families in their structure, and they are stronger for it. But as congregations grow in numbers and complexity, it becomes important to lay out relationships with a more explicit structure and lines of accountability.

Accountability is not a matter of power and authority, making some people more powerful and taking away power from others. Rather, the focus with accountability should be on how your congregation can achieve results and reach its goals.

The church is not called to simply exist. Instead, we are called to go and make disciples of all people. This gives ministry and mission purpose. These are tasks that can be measured and counted. They call us into accountability.

Use the "Delegating Responsibility" tool on pages 94-97 to consider the issues involved in delegating a task.

The ability to delegate is a key leadership skill.

Single reporting relationships

A youth worker attended a planning team meeting and agreed to a certain task. At a staff meeting later that week, the senior pastor had other ideas for the youth worker's time.

But at a meeting the following Monday, the congregation council had yet another plan for the youth worker. What should she do? To whom is she ultimately accountable? These types of dilemmas can arise when individuals, whether paid staff or volunteers, find themselves accountable to more than one person.

Individuals cannot be accountable to a group of people. It's also true that the more people who try to address accountability concerns with an individual, the less accountable that person becomes.

Accountability and delegation

Delegating responsibility and authority gives volunteers and paid staff members the tools they need to use their talents and gifts in mission and ministry. Accountability ensures the work stays on task and is aligned with the congregation's vision. Knowing the dynamics of responsibility, authority, and accountability can contribute greatly to the smooth functioning of the congregation.

Chapter 7

The Basics of Congregational Structure

But the Lord answered her, "Martha, Martha, you are worried and distracted by many things; there is need of only one thing. Mary has chosen the better part, which will not be taken away from her."

—Luke 10:41-42

As in any organization, it is exceedingly easy in the church to be distracted by many things. Bustling about to keep the lights on and the bills paid in our congregation, we may need to be reminded of Jesus' words to Martha amid our conversations about structure. As Christians, we have a mission to convey the gospel of Jesus Christ. We are the only human community set aside by God for that purpose. Organizational structure is not an end unto itself, but a means to facilitate that high calling from our Lord. Don't let focusing on your structure distract you from the mission!

Congregational structure

On the other hand, every organization, including a congregation, needs a structure if it is to be effective and efficient in carrying out its purpose. We've looked at some of the dynamics that operate within congregational structures. Now we will spend time looking at the practical implications of putting together a system that will work for your congregation.

The congregation

In the Evangelical Lutheran Church in America, the broadest expression of organization in the congregation is the congregation as a whole, which exercises authority through congregational meetings.

Governance and management

Authority to carry on the work of the church is divided into two main areas.

When the congregation is not in session at a duly called congregational meeting, authority to carry on the work of the church is divided into two main areas: governance and management. As you begin looking at the specifics of structure for your particular congregation, it will become important to define who is responsible for governance issues and who in the congregation is responsible for the management of the mission and ministry.

Governance is creating and maintaining the vision and the direction of the congregation, setting policies in place, carrying out fiduciary responsibilities, and guiding the congregation's affairs. Management is the process of planning, leadership development, organizing, and setting procedures (such as how purchases are made, how paid staff will be managed, and so forth) in place for the day-to-day operation of the congregation. Confusion often develops when these roles are reversed or not well understood.

Depending on the size of your congregation and its particular organizational structure, governance and management can be approached in a variety of ways as long as most of your congregation understands and accepts what is done. Your task is to help congregation members understand why these two roles need to be clearly defined and assigned a place in your structure.

Adaptability

Congregations that are adaptable can adjust to meet the needs of hurting people and carry out the vision. Adaptability depends on leaders who can think "outside the box" without falling into an "anything goes" mentality (chaos) and understand the value of stability and organization without micromanagement (rigidity). Adaptability also requires mutual understanding and acceptance of governance and management roles, shared values that are reflected in the mission and ministry of the congregation, and an organizational structure that supports the vision.

See "The Tower of Babel and Pentecost" on pages 98-99 for a Bible study on adaptability.

The office of the pastor

Other denominations provide for leadership in various ways, but in the ELCA the congregation chooses by vote at least one qualified person to be its pastor. The pastor's responsibilities are described in the constitution and further elaborated with the letter of call that is issued by the congregation. The authority that will be assigned to the role of the pastor is agreed upon as part of the call process or as part of a larger conversation about authority in the congregation. When this is not done, tension can result.

Officers and the council

Another structural element shared by Lutheran congregations is elected officers and a group of lay leaders called the congregation council. All other groups in the congregation relate in some way to the congregation council or, when delegated, to the pastor(s). The congregation council has "general oversight of the life and activities" (C12.04.) of the congregation on behalf of all the members.

Standing committees

The Model Constitution for Congregations of the ELCA describes five committees as essential for ELCA congregations. An Executive Committee is made up of the officers and pastor(s) of the congregation. There are three other standing committees: a Nominating Committee, an Audit Committee, and a Staff Support Committee. In addition, when a pastoral vacancy occurs, a Call Committee is set up to select and recommend a candidate, either to the council or to a meeting of the whole congregation.

Other than these standing committees, how you organize your particular congregation should be determined by your congregation's strategic planning process and vision. For example, in some congregations in the United States structure consists of the congregation as a whole, the pastor, and officers and council members. Specific tasks are taken care of by guilds or service groups, but there is no committee or planning team structure.

Some congregations have a board of directors instead of a council and may assign the management of all missions and ministry to a board of ministries chaired by the pastor. Some make use of voter assemblies, which are frequent (monthly or quarterly) meetings of the whole congregation, similar to a "town meeting." Whether your congregation requires a structure that is simple or complex, the most important element is the congregation's vision or sense of mission.

Structuring for mission

The reason many congregations have planning teams, committees, or other structures is to help the congregation operate. In some settings, the public school, volunteer fire department, and congregation might have been the only institutions around at one time and people might have worked to ensure the well being of these institutions and the larger community. This is less likely to be the case now. Few people today will get excited about ministry if the only purpose for structure seems to be maintaining the organization. When a community surrounding a congregation does not see the congregation as essential to its well-being or when other institutions have become the glue that holds the community together, people are less inclined to support the congregation with their time and energy, especially if the congregation does not allow members to use their passions and gifts in life-giving and affirming ways.

When members get involved in other styles of ministry or when no one can remember the last time the ministry of the congregation moved someone to become a disciple of Jesus Christ, it is difficult to explain to faithful people why they should invest their time and energy to support the congregation's structure.

In congregations with a strong sense of mission, however, ministry grows. Some consultants have advocated a mission-centered structure, which reflects an intentional effort to make disciples. Others advocate for a focus on health and wellness, or learning ministries, or other concerns. Whatever the mission focus, congregational leaders need to foster a unifying vision (or a sense of urgent mission) that draws people to a future that matters to them.

People will not respond to visions that are only disguised appeals to maintain the institution. A compelling vision is outward-looking and service-oriented and has genuine significance. For a vision to be truly unifying, it must capture the imagination, not just the intellect. It must awaken enthusiasm, not just passive agreement. It must point to a future in which the congregation makes a real difference in people's lives.

Many congregations with a clear sense of mission have strong leaders, clergy and lay, who articulate the vision. But true leaders know that they can never impose their will on those who follow. Leadership is a function of relationships and trust as much as it is about competency and skills. When leaders have articulated a compelling vision for the congregation, there is little doubt in the minds of members and visitors as to why the congregation exists.

The congregation's focus for mission may arise from within the congregation or in response to needs around it.

- In one congregation, the mission or reason for being might be: "To give the children in the neighborhood hope for the future by providing for their safety, helping them develop their potential, and introducing them to the gospel of Jesus Christ." Perhaps in a congregation near a research center, the reason for being is: "To provide a place where intellectual discoveries can be discussed and shaped in the context of the biblical tradition."

For more discussion on mission, see *Our Mission: Discovering God's Call to Us.*

- In a community undergoing economic upheaval, the reason for being might be: "To provide a place for renewing hope, strengthening families, and building skills for living in a changed situation."

- In a community with an older population, the reason for being might be: "To bring spiritual, physical, and emotional health to residents in our community."

- And in a community with lots of adults in their 20s, 30s, and 40s, the reason for being might be: "To help people find meaning and hope through hearing and learning the scriptures."

Congregations with a clear purpose view their structure, whatever it might be, as a way to support and extend their mission.

Whatever the mission focus or organizing principle, congregations with a clear purpose view their structure, whatever it might be, as a way to support and extend their mission. Property maintenance is seen as a way to eliminate barriers to evangelism or learning. Worship services and small groups are understood as ways to shape people's lives in light of the congregation's vision, rather than as ends in themselves. Education, stewardship, finance, and social ministry are viewed as specialized applications of what the congregation is about, and leaders and planning team members conduct their work accordingly. Some congregations have found ways to strengthen their ministry by linking the work of these various ministry areas together.

Congregations with clear, significant mission tend to be congregations where:

- the needs, hopes, dreams, and aspirations of the congregation's members and visitors have formed the vision;

- the ministry of the congregation takes into account all of the members' lives, not just the few hours a week they may spend in the church building;

- caring and committed leaders reinforce the vision with their words and actions; and

- the organizational structure supports the vision and provides people with an opportunity to fulfill it.

Four models for congregational structure

Your congregation's ministry can be organized effectively in many ways. There is not a model that should be used in all congregations or an ideal number of planning teams or committees that must be formed. The best structure will be one that allows your congregation to focus on mission and carry out its vision.

Most consultants who work in congregations conclude that it is unwise for congregations to depend too heavily on standing committees or planning teams if there are fewer than about 350 members. Take your congregation's culture, size, and resources into account so that the number of people available can maintain the structure you develop.

In the rest of this chapter, we will look at four models for congregational structure: council-based, compromise, staff-intensive, and committee-based.

A council-based structure

In smaller congregations it is common for the congregation council to function as a committee of the whole. In a council-based structure, the council may consist of an executive committee (the officers and pastor) and one or two members elected to care for each specified ministry area. Functions that are carried out by planning teams or committees in other congregations are instead functions of the congregation council. Working groups are formed as necessary and are viewed as committees of the congregation council. Members of the council are given responsibility for specific ministry areas and become the chairs or liaisons for those planning teams or committees.

In this model, it is important to provide a variety of ways for people to be involved in the congregation's work. Rather than expecting people to become involved only by serving on the council, try to identify tasks that can be enjoyed by people who have focused interests and prefer more hands-on involvement.

A diagram of a council-based structure appears on page 100.

A compromise structure

The structure can grow as the size of the congregation grows.

The smaller congregation that is becoming too large for the council-based structure can create a few planning teams that function more independently, relieving the council of direct responsibility for these areas. There is no reason to force the congregation into a certain number of planning teams. The structure can grow as the size of the congregation grows.

Similarly, the mid-sized or larger congregation with declining membership should consider combining some planning teams to reflect more accurately the number of people available to serve.

A diagram of a compromise structure appears on page 101.

Eight functions often assigned to planning teams or committees are education, evangelism, finance, property, social ministry, stewardship, worship and music, and youth. In a compromise structure, these functions can be combined in many ways. Here is one way to do this:

Spiritual Formation Team	Community Relations Team	Management Team
Education	Evangelism	Finance
Worship/Music	Social Ministry	Property
	Youth	Stewardship

If these functions are combined in your congregation, be sure to develop a coherent rationale for the structure so there is no confusion about the type of work each planning team will do. You might also create somewhat larger planning teams than is usually recommended, perhaps pulling together as many as 10 people to reflect the broader range of tasks to be managed.

A staff-intensive structure

The staff-intensive structure is used most often by large congregations or those that are making serious efforts to attain a very large membership. In addition, some church growth experts advise newly developed congregations to put their money into staff rather than buildings. (Volunteers may fill positions temporarily until the congregation can afford to pay staff members.)

We live in a complex society where professionals meet many of our needs for child care, health, recreation, services for elderly people, and so on. Many people are willing to pay for quality services, equipment, and trained personnel to assist them in these areas.

There are many ways for congregations to adapt to this cultural context. Some congregations have adopted a staff-intensive structure that focuses on the pastor and other paid staff members. In this model, there are no standing committees or planning teams, and most of the congregation's day-to-day operation is carried out by staff members rather than by volunteers. Responsibility for the management of ministry falls to those who have been hired for that purpose.

Hiring staff, even on a part-time basis, does not eliminate the need for volunteers. In a staff-intensive structure, volunteers are freed up to spend time on ministries rather than on management, planning, and recruitment. Volunteer opportunities tend to be for short-term projects, rather than for participation in standing committees that take on complex administrative tasks. The staff recruits members of the congregation (or even repeat visitors as they look for a new church home) to work on task groups or teams for a short period of time and for tasks of narrow focus. Staff members enhance the work of volunteers by creating opportunities for people to invest their time and energy in more specialized aspects of ministry that use their passions and gifts.

A diagram of a staff-intensive structure appears on page 102.

Hiring staff does not eliminate the need for volunteers.

In practical terms, this structure requires that a congregation make a deliberate effort, as rapidly as financially possible, to hire staff members to manage specialized functions as needed. Some congregational leaders may strongly object to a staff-intensive structure, preferring one in which members of the congregation exercise more direct leadership of the church's program. For many congregations, however, this structure simply expands what has become an accepted practice.

In this model a senior pastor, lead pastor, or executive pastor assumes the role of senior staff manager. Many pastors have not yet been trained in how to attract and build a quality team of staff members, manage workflow, define functions for job descriptions, set goals with staff members and teams, or evaluate results. As a result, some congregations have found it helpful to hire a professional staff manager or to call an executive pastor who has training and experience managing a complex staff situation.

With the staff-intensive structure comes a different understanding of the role of the congregation council. Members of the council are selected because they are leaders with gifts for vision, understanding and making policy decisions, and carrying out fiduciary responsibilities. The council spends most of its time thinking about the future of the congregation, examining long-range plans, and working with the staff to help define growing areas of ministry. In this structure, time and money should be set aside for leaders to have regular retreats and continuing education opportunities.

Critics of the staff-intensive approach to organization say that it encourages people to think of the congregation as an institution, rather than as a community, and to view the congregation's members as clients or customers, rather than as a family. Defenders of the approach, however, argue that seeing the congregation as an institution and the members as partners in ministry is a valid response to our present cultural context.

A committee-based structure

A diagram of a committee-based structure is on page 103.

While it is unwise for congregations with fewer than approximately 500 members to depend too heavily on planning teams or standing committees, larger congregations should have adequate support for a committee-based structure. The number of planning teams to establish depends on your congregation's vision and resources. Keep in mind that asking people to accomplish an impossible task diminishes their enthusiasm for the work of the congregation.

When congregations develop complex structures that cannot be maintained by the number of people available, the main focus for

Many people would say that these phrases have nothing in common. Committees have become known as places where time is wasted, nothing is accomplished, or power struggles erupt.

As seen in previous chapters, this may be due to communication problems, undefined responsibility and authority, a lack of focus, or misunderstandings about what committees are supposed to do. In some cases, the leaders of a congregation choose a new course that a significant minority does not want to follow.

To build an effective committee-based structure in your congregation, you will need to determine how many planning teams you will need, how many people might serve on each team, what responsibilities and authority should be assigned, and how you will train leaders to conduct meetings.

What do the following phrases have in common?

- a sense of fulfillment

- getting things done

- short meetings

- excellent use of time

- the gospel proclaimed

- planning teams or committees

planning teams becomes simply finding people to fill all the empty slots. Eventually all the slots may be filled and meetings are scheduled, but no one is left with sufficient energy to do actual ministry!

In most cases, a planning team should function as a "single cell" group, which means that members are able to pay attention to each other's body language, attention level, role in the group, and so forth. Generally, eight is a maximum number of people who can function as a single cell, including the chair or other group leader and any permanent advisory members such as a pastor or staff person who relates to the team.

If only one or two people involved in planning, there will be insufficient diversity of backgrounds, personalities, and viewpoints to accomplish the task. Furthermore, this may be an indication that a particular ministry has insufficient support within the congregation. On the other hand, a larger team may need to subdivide at times so that members can become part of project teams or serve as liaisons to subcommittees.

In general, the right size for a planning team or committee is about six people. Note that this is an even number. There is no need to provide for a tie-breaking vote because the group usually will operate by consensus. Members do not need to arrive at a unanimous opinion about what needs to be done but should keep working on a proposal if the group is divided.

When a staff person is assigned to a planning team, issues of responsibility, authority, and accountability should be clearly spelled out. In most cases, planning teams cannot and should not manage staff members. The staff member should be accountable to a person, most likely the pastor, and not to the team or a personnel committee. Similarly, a staff person should not be assigned to keep an eye on a planning team. In this instance, other issues with communication or basic trust may be present.

A staff member could be assigned to bring certain expertise to the work of a planning team that has primary responsibility for a certain ministry. The staff member would then have advisory authority when working with the team.

Chapter 8

Planning Your Work

Whatever your task, put yourselves into it, as done for the Lord and not for your masters, since you know that from the Lord you will receive the inheritance as your reward; you serve the Lord Christ.

—Colossians 3:23-24

As a planning team or working group gains clarity about the congregation's mission, it also begins to formulate goals. A goal is a statement describing what you intend to accomplish during a period of time. Planning teams are all about setting goals, working toward the goals, and then evaluating how successful they have been in reaching the goals.

Setting goals and objectives

Each goal (or desired end result) needs an action plan, which begins with objectives. To form objectives, break down the goal into smaller tasks. If your goal is to sit atop a mountain, your objectives are to first to climb the foothills, then wade across the river, climb the sheer rock face, maneuver across the ice field, and scramble over the last precipice.

When you identify goals and objectives, try to figure out in advance what specific barriers you are likely to encounter and how you will overcome these barriers. Equip yourself with alternatives in case the river is too deep for wading. Decide whether you will bring along an ax to build a bridge or select a different route on your way to the mountain.

It is likely that your congregation already expects your planning team to do certain things to carry out part of the congregation's

Use the "Action Plan Worksheet" on pages 104-106 to identify goals and objectives for your congregation.

Develop *s-m-a-r-t* goals. Useful goals are *specific*, not general. They identify who, what, when, where, why, and how.

Goals should be *measurable*, dealing with things that can be counted such as tangible objects or observable human behavior. Goals should be *attainable* within the time allotted to achieve them, using the resources available.

Goals should be *realistic* so that they have a direct effect on the situations they are meant to address. Goals also should be *timely*, appropriate to the things that matter most now.

mission. For instance, "Conduct a Rally Day" might be a goal. The congregation's tradition demands it, the congregation's members expect it, and the team should provide it. But effective teams usually work with a basic idea long enough to articulate the real purpose for an activity. An education committee, for example, might state as one of its goals: "To provide an occasion in early September when children can be enrolled and have their enthusiasm reawakened for Sunday school." This goal clarifies the purpose of the undertaking and can help set the stage for creative planning, zealous recruitment of workers, and joyful participation by the congregation.

Brainstorming

No idea is ruled out as impossible, silly, unworkable, or outrageous.

In addition to adopting goals that satisfy expectations, it can be productive to spend some time envisioning alternative possibilities. Brainstorming is one of the most useful of all planning team activities. It involves discussing a subject from every possible angle, and no idea is ruled out as impossible, silly, unworkable, or outrageous. Some brainstorming sessions yield page after page of ideas that can be compressed and organized into manageable groupings and then reformulated into plans.

Not every brainstorming session yields a list of ideas. Participants may simply bounce ideas off each other until everyone suddenly realizes how to proceed and wonders why they did not all see the solution at the beginning. There are also times when brainstorming sessions are boring and stilted, and the planning team makes the valuable discovery that the subject is not very important and not worth much time and effort.

An annual planning calendar

The goals your planning team finally agrees to adopt probably will include a combination of those arising from others' expectations and those developed through your group's visioning process. Each goal needs a set of objectives, and perhaps a still more detailed action plan, which will lead to its fulfillment. Objectives must address two basic questions: Who will do the work, and when will it be done?

Whenever your planning team decides to do something, you need to be clear about who has agreed to follow through on each task and the deadline for completing it. This is a crucial step in planning and organizing your work. Your planning team might rely on minutes from meetings, a separate list of responsibilities, or an annual calendar for keeping track of your work.

No matter how you decide to track progress toward your goals, plan to review assignments and schedules at each meeting of your planning team. If you see that a project is getting behind schedule, you can decide whether to redistribute the work or adjust the schedule. Because altering one assignment or schedule might affect others, review all projects together in order to make all the necessary adjustments.

The annual budget

Your planning team is responsible for managing financial resources prudently while accomplishing your mission. If you are thorough in developing your objectives and action plans, it should be relatively easy for you to identify areas where you will need to budget funds.

Estimating expenses is an essential part of planning, and there are a number of ways to do this. In some cases, you will be able to contact several possible suppliers and secure competitive bids. Or you might consult an expert for advice on alternatives. Estimates may also be developed based on past history, the experience of other working groups in the congregation, or by consulting other congregations in the area.

Your planning team should consider the *cost benefit ratio* of the work it plans, which means looking at whether the payoff from the team's work is worth the human and financial resources devoted to it. This task is not as straightforward in congregations as it is for those who deal in more tangible commodities, like products for sale, and subjective judgments will need to be made.

Do your best to strike a balance with expenses.

Do your best to strike a balance with expenses, keeping the costs as low as possible and the benefits as great as possible. Skimping on a sanctuary remodeling project might result in the congregation worshiping for years in an environment that does not foster a sense of holiness for those who attend. Purchasing inferior office products because of a special discount might mean that you are stuck with equipment that requires frequent and expensive repairs. On the other hand, a planning team that hires the most expensive caterer in town might attract a few new people to the annual congregational dinner, but upon further reflection, people might agree that it would have been better to make a special donation to fight world hunger.

In many cases, the congregation council will be responsible for administering the annual budget of the congregation. The budget should include amounts allocated for the work of each planning team. The council should provide information about what funding is available as the team begins its work, and regularly update teams on their spending and any changes that need to be made due to cash flow. The planning team, in turn, should provide the council with reports on current and projected spending. A person who serves as a liaison between the planning team and the congregation council may be the channel for this reporting. In addition, each congregation should have a system of resource management and cost accounting, and every planning team should be held responsible for complying with these policies and procedures.

Preparing the annual budget

In many cases, the council prepares an annual budget as the congregation's fiscal year draws to a close. At this time, planning teams provide information about the financial resources needed to do their work. These budget requests should reflect the experience of the past year and projected needs based on plans for the coming year.

In addition to money needed for operating expenses and programs, your planning team might have other budget needs. Perhaps your work was hampered because something you needed was not available. As you evaluate your planning team's work, think about what kind of support you and others need in order to be more effective. The property team might be enthusiastic about the number of people responding to the congregation's programs, but also might notice that the congregation does not own enough chairs to accommodate everyone in the fellowship hall. The education planning team might want to set up multiple study groups but be hampered because the congregation owns only one videotape player. Or the staff support committee might conclude that the congregation's highly effective staff is stretched to its limit and that it is time to add another person. You will view these needs from the perspective of your planning team and its work, but your observations might be shared by others and could be important for the whole organization.

The annual report

In the Evangelical Lutheran Church in America, each congregation holds an annual meeting of its voting members. This meeting is the highest authority within the congregation and provides time for a congregation to elect officers, adopt a budget, and hear reports from each planning team. It can be an opportunity to celebrate the achievements of the year, recognize the people who helped make these things happen, and build consensus about the congregation's plans to witness and serve in the coming year.

The pastor, treasurer, financial secretary, council president, and the chairs of each planning team or working group may submit a printed report prior to the annual meeting. If this is the case in your congregation, your planning team should decide who is best equipped to write your report. Here are some things to consider:

- *Focus on goals.* Boldly say, "Here's what we decided to accomplish, here's what we did to get there, and here's the benefit to the kingdom of God that we achieved." It is actions, not intentions, that count. Measurable results, not hopes, contribute to growth.

- *Give glory to God.* Point to what is different now compared to a year ago.

- *Be honest.* If you accomplished little or nothing, be frank about that. The worst possible mistake is to try to take credit for something that did not happen or that was accomplished by someone else.

- *Use people's names.* (Make sure not to forget anyone.) This is a way to recognize the contributions of the women and men who exemplify what you are trying to accomplish. These people can serve as models for others.

- *Be results-oriented.* Use active verbs to tell the congregation what you did.

- *Use short sentences and simple words.* Describe the highlights the way your activities might get reported in *USA Today*.

- *Use graphics.* Develop line graphs and bar charts to illustrate trends in attendance or participation, growth in accomplishments, and achievement of measurable results.

- *Suggest further development.* Your report should suggest new directions for your planning team. Although new members of a planning team might take it in another direction, you should encourage the congregation to keep expanding its ministry.

In addition to the printed report, many congregations provide time for oral reports at the annual meeting of the congregation. Here are two possibilities to consider.

- *Bring the reports to life.* Use slides or video to give people the feeling of being involved. Show people the results. Be theatrical. Stage a skit. Illustrate statistics with live bodies. Choreograph a presentation that involves many people who can awaken interest and attract others to your work. Give away something tangible such as a button, balloon, or refrigerator magnet. Help people take the idea of your work home with them.

Help people take the idea of your work home with them.

- *Develop a mission fair.* Create visual displays of each planning team's work that people can walk around, touch, watch, listen to, and wonder about. Staff each booth with a person who can answer questions. Develop a way for people to register their interest through a sign-up sheet, petition, voting booth, graffiti board, or wishing well. Arrange to follow up with each person who responds, inviting those people to participate as appropriate in the work of your planning team during the next year.

Chapter 9

Working Together

Day by day, as they spent much time together in the temple, they broke bread at home and ate their food with glad and generous hearts, praising God and having the goodwill of all the people.

—Acts 2:46-47

A story about a visitor at church

After dropping off his daughter and son for Sunday school, the father would routinely pull over into an empty parking spot, pop open Sunday's paper, and wait until it was time to go. He'd never been much of a churchgoer, but with his divorce now final he figured the kids might get something out of their experience in the church. One Sunday he decided to wander into the church building for some fresh coffee. Another Sunday he sat down in the back of the hall and listened to a speaker during an adult Bible study.

Later on, he and his children went into a worship service together. Six months later, these ongoing prompts from the Holy Spirit led to his baptism as an adult. The passing of another six months found him serving on the stewardship planning team, his first introduction to a small group in the church. As someone newly called into the public life of a congregation, planning the upcoming stewardship dinner and making sure the festivities were adequately staffed was not his motivation for being in a meeting one night a month. He was there because the meetings always started with biblical insight linked to personal reflection and ended with prayer. His life was engaged by the power of a small group.

Planning teams as small groups

Planning teams, committees, and other working groups might not immediately come to mind when you think about small groups in your congregation. Many congregations have rediscovered the power of small groups, especially as ways to gather people together to grow as disciples of Jesus Christ. These groups are often called discipleship groups. Support groups and recovery groups are other types of small groups.

Most members of your congregation are already over-booked and weighed down by life. They are looking for community and renewal, not another night out for a business meeting. A 60-minute business meeting can contain time for prayer, gathering conversation, and biblical reflection while still leaving plenty of time for task management. One effective resource to help grow your planning teams into small groups is *Growing Together: Spiritual Exercises for Church Committees*, which is part of the Congregational Leader Series.

Effective chairs

Understanding the importance of feeding the heart, mind, and spirit of planning team members will help you build groups that matter to participants. But it's also important that people don't walk away thinking the rest of the meeting was a waste of time. Planning teams vary widely in how they go about their work. There is no single right style, but striking a balance between meeting the needs of members and productively carrying out the tasks at hand requires leadership.

A meeting can contain time for prayer, gathering conversation, and biblical reflection while still leaving plenty of time for task management.

One important key is the choice of a person to chair the planning team. The chair is responsible for calling and facilitating meetings, overseeing administrative details, coordinating members' contributions, and providing for communication with others such as the congregation council and pastor. The chair should not

There are several different ways that chairs of planning teams can be chosen:

- A member elected to the congregation council may automatically become the chair of a planning team.

- The nominating committee, congregation council, coordinator for volunteers, or pastor may specifically ask a person to serve as the chair. This person would be selected because of his or her interest, experience, gifts, and skills.

- Each planning team may select or elect its own chair.

try to do all the work but should make sure that the work gets done. The best chairs have skills in dealing with people as well as administration.

There are strengths and weaknesses to each method for selecting a chair, but in every case, congregations should look for the best possible chairs in order to provide for the strongest planning teams. The bylaws of the congregation should clarify how planning team chairs are chosen.

Conducting meetings

To conduct efficient meetings that are satisfying to the participants, begin with a clear agenda. Prepare the agenda about a week before the meeting and send it to participants as a reminder of the meeting and items they need to prepare. Review the agenda at the beginning of the meeting, adding, deleting, or rearranging items as the team members see fit. Good agendas include a time estimate for each item of business. It is best to start with a few easy items that can be addressed quickly. Then, move to more difficult items. After decisions have been reached, introduce items that are for discussion only. Be sure to allow time on the agenda for each person to report on work for which he or she is responsible.

Never let a meeting go longer than 90 minutes without a break. In general, two hours should be the maximum time for a meeting, with a break at the midpoint. There is seldom any reason for a meeting to last longer than three hours. If it must last that long, ask group members in advance for their consent.

The chair's role is to facilitate the discussion and decision-making process, not to dominate it. Strong leaders are always willing to let others lead discussions or present particular agenda items when appropriate. Each person has both the right and the obligation to participate fully. Members should respect differing viewpoints and willingly hear the opinions of others. Decisions usually should be made by consensus, which depends on mutual respect and strong communication. Effective chairs can encourage such respect by drawing out comments from some people and diplomatically keeping others from dominating discussions.

The chair's role is to facilitate the discussion and decision-making process.

Planning teams usually meet monthly, although there may be times during the year when they need to meet more often or less often than that. At the end of a meeting, there should be a statement of the individual responsibilities or follow-up actions each person has agreed to take, as well as a listing of items that will be on the next agenda.

Periodically, it is also helpful for the group to discuss whether there are any barriers that prevent the meetings from being as effective as the members would like them to be. Evaluating how the planning team is functioning is as important as evaluating the work for which the planning team is responsible. This evaluation can be done at the close of each meeting.

Providing clear expectations

Even if the planning team members are all skilled and committed to their work, they will find their task frustrating if they have been given a false impression of the scope and responsibilities of their group's work. Here are three common examples of unclear expectations:

1. The scope of the work is misrepresented, usually in a misguided attempt to minimize the work involved in order to get people to agree to serve.

   Example: The people who asked to serve on Bethel's education committee weren't told they would need to help with teach recruitment, even though the number of Sunday school teachers had been inadequate for the past three years.

2. The informal power structure of the congregation does not match the formal or official lines of authority.

   Example: Members of the stewardship planning team at Trinity put in hours of work developing a year-round stewardship program, which they believed was within the scope of their responsibility. When they presented an informational report to the congregation council, it was summarily vetoed. The stewardship planning team later found out later that decisions in this area ultimately were made only by the pastor, the president of the women's organization, and the congregation's biggest contributor.

3. Members of the planning team receives no guidance, resources, or recognition.

   Example: At St. Andrew's, the evangelism team received no information about their responsibilities. The members, wanting to be responsible, arrived at their own definition of their work. They attended workshops on becoming a mission-oriented church and decided to implement a hospitality-based welcoming program. Some members of the congregation later hinted that members of the planning team had failed to fulfill their responsibilities.

One way to clarify the roles and responsibilities is to provide job descriptions for planning teams and their members. These descriptions could be prepared by your congregation council or by a group established to work on structure and organization.

First, a general description should outline what the congregation expects of all planning team members and what these members can expect from the congregation.

Second, create specific job descriptions for each of the planning teams. Each description will contain information that should be communicated to all those asked to serve on that particular planning team:

- the purpose or mission of the group

- the membership (including the number of members, how they are selected, and any advisory members)

- an outline of team responsibilities

- the time commitment and term of office

- any subcommittees for which the group is responsible, expectations for skill development, or attendance at training events

- the individuals or groups to whom the team is accountable

You also might include the budget and a copy of your congregation's procedures for spending large sums or making unbudgeted expenditures.

In addition, it is important to take time for discussion within each planning team about its responsibilities and how the congregation's mission applies to the team. (Ideally, a strategic planning process has already taken place, a vision for the congregation has been identified, and leaders have organized the congregation's total mission into areas that can be handled by separate planning teams.) You may discover that not everyone on your planning team is reading the mission statement the same way. Or you might

A sample description of expectations for planning team members is available on pages 107-109.

See *Our Mission: Discovering God's Call to Us* for more information on congregational mission statements.

decide that from a practical standpoint, the mission statement is not achievable or that its scope needs to be narrowed to accommodate your situation. Once understanding and acceptance have been attained, the group is much more likely to be productive as well as helpful to the congregation's overall vision and mission.

Chapter 3 Tool

Keys to Hospitality

All members of the congregation

- Be friendly. Speak to people cordially and make them feel welcome.

- Smile at people. Work to make this a natural part of your life.

- Look people in the eye when you speak to them.

- Be considerate of people's feelings.

- Have a genuine interest in people.

- Get to know one new person by name each Sunday. Call people by name.

- Think of ways to help people before they ask.

- Become familiar with the facility and know where everything is.

- Be enthusiastic. Tell visitors about upcoming events and invite them to go with you.

Greeters

- Before the service, stand near your assigned entrance. Be close enough so you can reach people quickly but far enough away so that they do not feel smothered by your approach.

- Offer a handshake and a warm smile to members and visitors alike, introducing yourself by name to those people who do not know you.

- Ask visitors for their names, welcome them, and ask if you can help them in any way. As appropriate, direct or escort them to the nursery, Sunday school classes, or whatever else they might need, making introductions as appropriate.

- After the service has started, look for people who seem to be having trouble following the service. Give them worship books open to the correct hymn or page.

- Greet visitors during the sharing of the peace. Walk and talk with them as you leave the service.

- Introduce visitors to your friends or acquaintances during coffee hour.

Ushers

- Stand near your assigned entrance to the sanctuary.

- Offer worshipers a bulletin, smiling and looking them in the eye as you do so.

- Be alert for worshipers who appear to need further direction or assistance and ask if you can help.

- Pay attention to the service and the congregation.

- Know where seating is still available so you can quickly locate seats for latecomers.

- Watch for disturbances and deal with them.

- Use positive phrases to give instructions. For example, instead of saying, "You can't go in now," say, "We will seat you in just a moment."

Information booth greeters

- Be in the booth 15 minutes before the service begins.

- Read through worship bulletins or newsletters when you arrive for up-to-date information about upcoming events.

- Focus on visitors and initiate conversation with them: "Hi, my name is _____. How are you doing? May I help you with anything?" Get names and contact information for follow up.

- Offer newsletters, brochures, and other information to visitors.

- If possible, direct or escort visitors to the nursery, Sunday school classes, or wherever else they might need to go, making introductions as appropriate.

- Remain at the booth 10 minutes into the service.

- Be aware that visitors will either be very early or late, since they aren't accustomed to timing the drive or finding a parking place at your church.

Nursery attendants

- Be in the nursery 20 minutes before the service begins.

- As children arrive, warmly greet each child and parent or guardian, making introductions as needed.

- Be friendly and reassuring to members and visitors, explaining nursery routines and procedures as needed and answering questions.

Chapter 3 Tool

Seeing Our Congregation through New Eyes

Visitors

Ask several members of the congregation council, your planning team, or others to interview several individuals or families that have recently visited your congregation. Arrange to conduct these interviews face-to-face if possible. Keep a written record of responses to questions such as these:

- How did you find out about our congregation?

- Why did you decide to visit?

- How difficult (or easy) was it to locate the church?

- Describe your first visit. Did the church itself feel inviting? Why or why not? Did you feel welcome? Why or why not?

- What was your overall impression of the experience?

- What did you find at our congregation that you were looking for? What were you looking for that you did not find?

- If you were a part of our congregation, what would you seek to change in order to make it more inviting and accessible to newcomers?

At a subsequent meeting of your planning team, read the responses aloud.

- What similarities do you see in the responses?

- Do you discover anything new in these responses?

- What do the visitors need that they are finding? How can those assets be enhanced?

- What do the visitors need that they are not finding? How can those needs be addressed?

- Are any actions needed to improve the visibility, accessibility, or hospitality of the congregation? If so, how can you plan and carry through on those actions?

People who are in some contact with the congregation

First, brainstorm a list of the members served by the congregation: children in Sunday school, worship attendees, shut-ins, and so on. Make the list as long as possible.

Next, brainstorm a list of everyone who has any contact at all with the congregation but is not a member: the mail carrier, delivery person, people who attend meetings in the building, those who cut the grass, Girl Scout and Boy Scout troops, and so on. Make the list as long as possible.

- What are the similarities between the people on the two lists?

- What are the differences between the people on the two lists?

- Are there any physical or emotional barriers preventing the people on the second list from visiting and joining your congregation?

Neighbors

Draw a picture of the average person who lives in your congregation's neighborhood but is not a member of a community of faith. If your neighborhood is diverse and has more than one distinct group, draw more than one person.

Describe the ranges of age, income, education, employment status, church background, and so forth of the neighbors(s).

- What are your neighbors' needs? How do these needs compare to those of your congregation's current members? Are you currently organized to meet these needs?

- Realistically speaking, how open is your congregation to doing whatever it might take to welcome your neighbors into your fellowship?

Chapter 5 Tool

The Burning Bush

Bible Study

The smooth functioning of any organization, including a congregation, requires clear and precise communication. Everyone involved needs to understand what is to be accomplished and commit to carrying out the work. Speaking only for yourself (using "I" language) and identifying your own assumptions and preconceived ideas can prevent misunderstandings, build trust, and improve communication.

Read Exodus 3:1-15

* God has a task to assign Moses but first must secure Moses' understanding and acceptance. Give examples of God using "I" language in this story. What perceptions does God share with Moses (verses 7-9) to help Moses understand the need for the task? What does God want? What would God like from Moses?

* Does Moses speak for himself in this story? What do you think Moses wants? What does Moses feel in the presence of God? Does he share this information?

* What do you think God means by saying, "I am who I am," or "I will be what I will be"?

* Have you had any "burning bush" experiences in your life? If so, how did you come to understand what God wanted? What did it mean to accept the task or journey?

Delegating Responsibility

This tool can be used in two ways:

1. To consider the many factors involved in delegating a task.

2. To provide valuable information to an individual or group taking on a task.

Description of the task

How does the task fit with the congregation's mission statement?

_____

_____

_____

_____

Where did the idea originate?

_____

_____

List the various steps required in this task. Include a completion date for each step.

_____

_____

_____

_____

_____

What is the job description for this task?

_____

_____

_____

_____

Responsibility

What type of responsibility will the individual or group have?

- Responsibility for completion

_____

- Responsibility for input or advice

_____

- Responsibility for service

_____

Authority

Are there informal authorities for the individual or group taking on the task? If so, who are they?

_____

_____

_____

Are there defined formal authorities for the individual or group taking on the task? If so, where are these spelled out?

_____

_____

_____

Will the individual or group have sufficient authority to carry out the work and complete the task or project?

_____

_____

_____

Accountability

To whom is the individual or group accountable?

_____

_____

How and when will progress reports be made?

_____

_____

_____

Resources

What resources will be needed to complete the task or project? How will they be obtained?

_____

_____

_____

What sort of training would be helpful?

_____

_____

_____

Evaluation

How and when will the work be evaluated?

_____

_____

_____

For future planning, how will you collect suggestions for improving the process from the individual or group carrying out the task?

_____

_____

_____

_____

Chapter 7 Tool

The Tower of Babel and Pentecost

Bible Study

Congregations that are adaptable can adjust to meet the needs of hurting people and carry out the vision. They maintain a healthy balance between an "anything goes" mentality (chaos) and micromanagement (rigidity). Their organizational structures support mission and ministry and can change if necessary.

Read Genesis 11:1-9

- In this story, why did people build the Tower of Babel?

- How might the Tower of Babel have influenced the people's relationships with one another and with God?

- What effect did the confusion of the language (chaos) have on the people?

Read Acts 2:1-21

At Pentecost, each person heard the disciples' message in their own language.

- What would happen in your congregation if everyone heard and understood the mission and vision?

For discussion

- Would you characterize your congregation as adaptable? Is there a balance between chaos and rigidity, or is one of these predominant?

- What effect does the adaptability of your congregation have on your mission and ministry?

- What are some ways your organizational structure may change as it adapts to the congregation's vision?

Chapter 7 Tool

A Council-Based Structure

In this example, the pastor and the congregation council president, vice president, secretary, and treasurer serve on the Executive Committee. The congregation council consists of the Executive Committee plus 10 members of the congregation (two each coordinating worship and music, learning ministries, witness and evangelism, community outreach and social ministry, and stewardship). The individuals or groups responsible for ministry areas would periodically come to council meetings to report on their work and their needs.

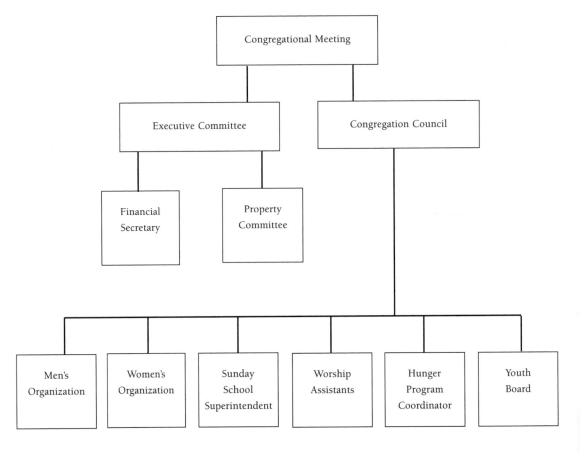

Our Structure: Carrying Out the Vision, copyright © Augsburg Fortress. May be reproduced for local use.

Chapter 7 Tool

A Compromise Structure

Congregations becoming too large for a council-based structure but too small to be fully committee-based might adopt a structure similar to this one. The congregation in this example has chosen to have the council elect officers from within the council membership.

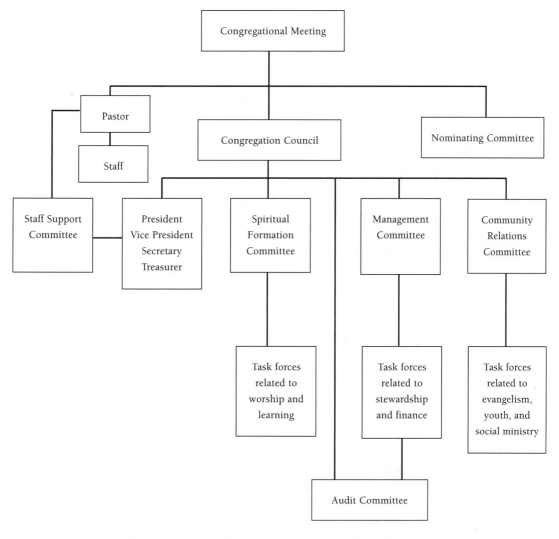

Our Structure: Carrying Out the Vision, copyright © Augsburg Fortress.
May be reproduced for local use.

Chapter 7 Tool

A Staff-Intensive Structure

Framed boxes = paid positions

Solid lines = direct accountability

Broken lines = liaison relationships

There are many ways to set up a staff-intensive structure. In this example, the paid staff is accountable to the congregation and council through the pastor, while volunteer committee members are accountable to the council. The staff and the committees have liaison relationships with one another.

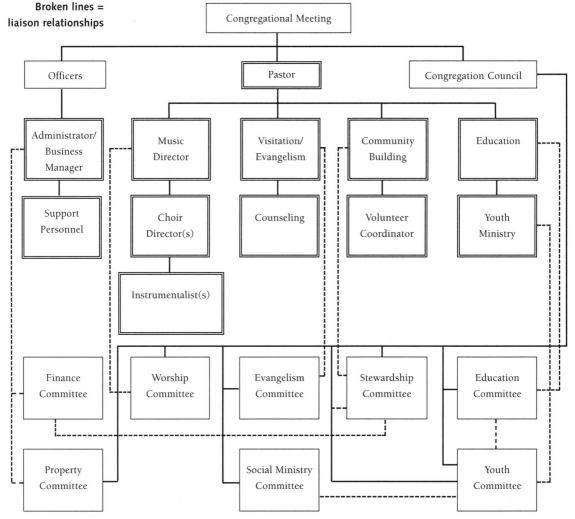

Our Structure: Carrying Out the Vision, copyright © Augsburg Fortress. May be reproduced for local use.

Chapter 7 Tool

A Committee-Based Structure

In a committee-based structure, the congregation council might consist of the pastor, officers, and chair of each committee or planning team. Another option is for each council member to serve as a liaison to one or two committees. Each committee would have its own chair and submit only written reports to the council.

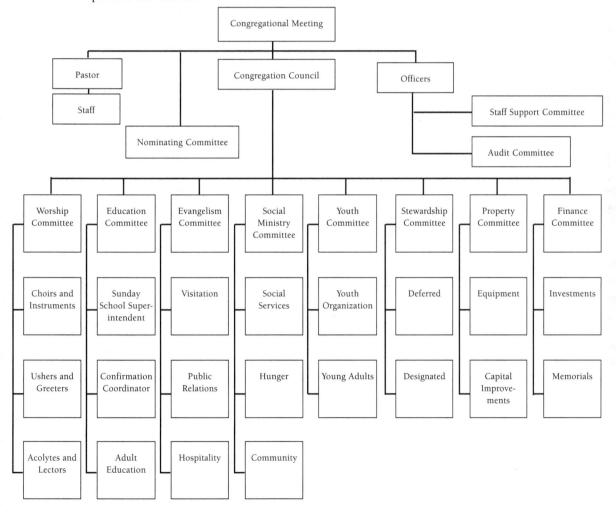

Our Structure: Carrying Out the Vision, copyright © Augsburg Fortress. May be reproduced for local use.

Chapter 8 Tool

Action Plan Worksheet

1. Write down one of your congregation's goals.

_____

_____

_____

_____

_____

2. List the steps or objectives involved in reaching this goal.

_____

_____

_____

_____

_____

3. How will this be done?

_____

_____

_____

_____

_____

_____

4. Why will this be done?

_____

_____

_____

_____

5. Who will have the primary responsibility for implementing the steps?

_____

_____

_____

_____

6. Which resources will be used? Identify the financial resources, equipment, and so on that are needed. Are these resources available now or will they need to be obtained?

_____

_____

_____

_____

7. When and where will the steps be completed? Identify the timeline for completion and (if needed) the location.

_____

_____

_____

_____

Evaluation

1. When will progress reports be given?

_____

_____

2. How will you know that the goal has been reached?

_____

_____

Chapter 9 Tool

Expectations of Planning Team Members

What the planning team can expect from the congregation

- The pastor(s), staff members, congregation council, members of other planning teams, and other leaders of the congregation will regularly pray for you and for the work of your planning team.

- The pastor(s) and other staff of the congregation will assist and cooperate with you in your work.

- Leaders of the congregation will provide a job description that describes the responsibilities you are asked to assume.

- The pastor(s) and officers will inform you in a clear and timely way of congregational policies and procedures that have a bearing on the work of your planning team.

- The congregation will take reasonable precautions to ensure that you will be safe while engaged in the work of the planning team or other work on the congregation's behalf.

- The congregation's budget will include money for carrying out the work of your planning team, and the congregation council will provide timely information concerning the status of income and expenditures, including any adjustments that are necessary.

- The congregation will pay for the expenses of the planning team's work.

- The pastor(s), executive committee, and congregation council will acknowledge your planning team's work so that the whole congregation can thank you for your efforts on behalf of our mission and ministry.

What the congregation expects of planning team members

- Pray regularly for the congregation, our pastor(s) and staff, the congregation council, and the other members of your planning team.

- Faithfully join our worshiping community to hear God's word and celebrate the sacraments.

- Undertake and evaluate the effectiveness of your planning team's work in light of the call to proclaim the gospel and the needs of the congregation.

- Attend meetings of your planning team regularly and be a full partner in discussion and decision-making.

- Complete all tasks you agree to undertake.

- Promote a congregational climate of peace and goodwill and, as differences and conflicts arise, endeavor to foster mutual understanding.

- Speak positively to members of the congregation and others about the work of your planning team and about the ministry and leadership of the whole congregation.

- Plan the work of the planning team in collaboration with other planning team members, and set goals and priorities that are in harmony with the mission and goals of the congregation as a whole.

- Take the initiative to maintain good communication with the pastor(s), staff, and other leaders of the congregation.

- Seek to involve as many members as possible in your planning team's work.

- Be a good steward of the resources of the congregation. Be wise and trustworthy in the use of financial resources for which your planning team is responsible.

- Carry out your functions with integrity, by conducting your work in an ethical and lawful way, taking responsibility for your own actions, and being charitable in the way you view the actions of others.

- Observe all relevant policies and procedures of the congregation when you conduct planning team business.

- Follow the policies of our congregation and denomination, as applicable, when you do your planning team's work.